In Balance
The Fundamentals of Ballet

In Balance
The Fundamentals of Ballet

Janice D. LaPointe-Crump
Texas Woman's University

wcb
Wm. C. Brown Publishers
Dubuque, Iowa

"To the one who has danced with most spirit."
inscription on Greek cup, ca. 500 B.C.

Consulting Editor—Aileene S. Lockhart

Contents

The spirit of motion.
University of Georgia.
(Stephen R. West,
photographer)

Preface

Are you a little anxious at the thought of entering the world of the dance? You are not alone. Each of us has faced the awesomeness and the mystery of the ballet class with eagerness yet with some fear. There is so much to learn at first! This book will assist you in the vital, crucial first steps. Your adventure begins within the rigors of a ritual with two hundred years of evolving traditions as its backbone. The movements you will learn are carefully stylized and unnatural in the sense of how we move in everyday life. Nineteenth century balletmaster, August Bournonville, wrote that "Dance is a beautiful art because it aims at the ideal, as much for plastic beauty, as for lyric and dramatic expression."[1]

Many dancers started taking lessons for diverse reasons. We often think only of those who seemed to have been born to dance, seeing on stage only the results of years of intensive training, physical aptitude, and months of rehearsing. Others, like the elegant Danish Erik Bruhn and the explosive American Edward Villella, were marched off to ballet class accompanying their sisters, or, as in the case of the incomparable English ballerina, Margot Fonteyn, they began because this was a proper pastime for little girls. Bruhn, Villella, and Fonteyn had to find a sense of purpose.

What unifies all successful dancers, however, has been that special effect which their studies of classical dance have had on their lives. The exhilaration of motion is like no other human experience, resulting in a heightened self awareness, confidence, discipline, and accomplishment.

Use this little book to reinforce what is being learned in your class. As a handbook first and foremost, it contains vocabulary, information, definitions, and performing cautions which are supplemental to the actual practice of the techniques experienced in the studio. Reviewing those steps learned in the class, their correct execution and notes on appropriate internal feelings will enhance the understanding and intellectual knowledge gained in the actual physical experiencing and putting-into-practice of these insights.

Entering the World of Ballet

The first chapter on dressing for the ballet, class etiquette, and alignment should be read prior to the first lesson. From there, the chapters begin with the theoretical concepts from which generations of teachers, gifted artists, and imaginative choreographers have expanded the dancer's vocabulary of movement and design. Whether your instructor gives a pre-barre warm-up is frequently a matter of individual preference, but you will probably be encouraged to "loosen up" before class begins. Chapter two describes a number of easy limbering activities from which you can create your own personal 10–15 minute preparation for each day's lesson.

Essential vocabulary and primary movements of the barre have been divided into two chapters beginning with those which you will encounter during the first lessons. Being burdened with too much information too soon can be overwhelming, inefficient in terms of immediate application. For that reason, barre and center practice have each been divided so that the student encounters only those kinds of materials which will be experienced during the first weeks of study. As the class progresses, more advanced techniques will be introduced gradually (perhaps not in the exact sequence given here). Those complex and demanding movements comprising more advanced barre practice are analyzed in chapter five.

Leaving the barre to face the mirrors for center work is called *au milieu*. A time for re-orientation of the mind and body in order to perform before an hypothetical audience seated just beyond the mirrors, or whatever wall the class faces should your studio not be equipped with mirrors, is discussed in chapter six. Since most beginner classes frequently practice elements of barre work in the center, only those new concepts, positions, facing directions, steps, and transitional movements you might perform during the critical first few months of training are described.

Turns, balances, poses, and more advanced jumps are introduced in both chapters six and seven. A separate chapter is devoted to the large jumps and turns which are usually executed in a series on a long diagonal. These techniques require great strength, muscular stamina, and coordination in order to do them safely and beautifully. Only a few may be practiced during the first year, but you should be aware of these movements since it is on the path toward learning these steps that you are headed.

All academic classical steps can be traced genealogically to three primary actions: *plié*— to bend, *elevé*— to rise, *battement*— straight leg beat. These elemental actions are the very core of classical technique; the ability to execute these fundamental movements correctly and consistently will relate directly to how well and how quickly you will be able to master more advanced steps. A progressive approach to the introduction of more advanced steps is the primary logic for this book. Emphasized throughout is a balanced use of the body, structurally and mechanically, coupled with an intellectual vs. emotional understanding of posture, movements, and poses comprising the vocabulary of classical ballet dancing—hence the title of this book.

What will be practiced and performed has been established by people, people who for one reason or another found themselves in the profession of performing with the one instrument common to all people in all civilizations—the body. All "art emanates from humanity," Karel Shook, the great contemporary teacher, has affirmed.[2] Knowing how various eras felt about the body as an instrument, and dance as a theatrical art form, is a very important link for your understanding of classical dance. Aesthetic values evolved, even as they do today, to provide dancers with necessary forms, poses, rhythmic patterns, technical challenges, performing repertoire, and standards for artistic accomplishment. This pageant from the past and present times, found in chapters eight and nine, establishes a proper historical framework for your explorations into the world of classical dance, the ballet.

Additional reading sources have been provided in a selected bibliography. Further appendices include a list of facing directions and an extensive, topical glossary of balletic terminology. Each chapter culminates with a short series of study questions to help you remember the important concepts.

Your training in classical dance will be exciting and rewarding; sound mental, aesthetic, and physical values will become a part of your life. As your body moves in harmony with the music, you will develop precision, endurance, discipline, patience, a sense of personal freedom, movement skills, and the self-confidence which come from an holistic mind and body experience.

Acknowledgments

A hearty thank you to the following beautiful people who have made such valuable contributions to this book: Diann Emerson, dancer; Jennifer Collins, Katie Rae, and Theresa Meaney, photographers; Gail N. Crump, illustrator/collaborator; Kathleen Tenniswood, editorial assistant and typist; and especially Aileene S. Lockhart, editor, without whose gentle encouragement this book would not have been written.

To the following list of schools who so graciously agreed to permit photograhs to be included, a note of gratitude: Ballet West—Christiansen Academy—Virginia Greenlaw; Dallas Arts Magnet High School—Rosann Cox; Florida School of the Arts—Christian Faust; Louisiana State University—Gaye Meyer; The Ohio State University—Vera Blaine; Texas Christian University—Lisa Fusillo; The Texas Woman's University—Jane Mott; the University of Georgia—Lynn Leopold; and the University of Illinois at Champaign-Urbana—Patricia Knowles; Brigham Young University—Sandra B. Allen.

In Balance
The Fundamentals of Ballet

Correcting body placement.
Texas Christian University.
(Linda Kaye, photographer)

Opening the Door

The Language of Classical Ballet

1

G. B. L. Wilson, in his *Dictionary of Ballet,* has defined ballet as a theatrical entertainment including group or solo dancing performed to some kind of musical accompaniment on a stage and dressed out with appropriate costumes, scenery, and lighting. So generalized is this statement that it may be difficult to gain a proper sense of why ballet is *ballet* and not another kind of dance.

Definitions written by earlier dancing masters will provide a more exact view. Over 200 years ago, Jean Georges Noverre described ballet as "a series of pictures connected one with the other. . . ."[1] Ballet is not merely a conglomeration of held poses. Those pictures, of which Noverre spoke, are the very heart of ballet or classical dancing. Founded upon ordered qualities, singing lyricism, and natural harmony of which the human body is capable, ballet technique must be supremely visible in a dance if it is to be called ballet. In 1831, Carlo Blasis demanded that "genius must be restrained by rules, and nature should be regulated by art."[2]

Whether a ballet reveals an abstract linear architecture of the body as in George Balanchine's *Apollo* or an almost slapstick, off-balanced witty view of modern man in Twyla Tharp's *Push Comes to Shove* is not the issue. While the primary rules of movement were devised in the courts of Italy in the 16th and 17th centuries, still these dances are balletic because of their reliance upon classical technique as the basis of the motion. That movement foundation encompasses an ingrown sense of ethereal free flight from earth, fluidity, geometry, precision, variety, and a decided hint of regal elegance. No matter how earthy or contemporary the theme of a ballet, like Agnes deMille's *Rodeo* or Frederick Ashton's *Monotones,* the body will reveal its classical inclination and the choreographer will use the dancers in a very special manner. Women on pointe move in a manner very different from their barefoot sisters, and men will never entirely lose their role as the gallant cavalier while they dance with the ballerina.

When learning the technical repertoire, you will be participating in developing the tools which form the very heart of ballet as an art form. The dance truly begins to flower in the studio. Learning to become artistically sensitive as well as physically skilled is a vital part of the dance experience. Be constantly aware of the musical, design, and dramatic values of the various movements practiced at first singly and then in combination. The lines the body creates do not, for example, end at the finger and toe tips. They radiate in lines far beyond the finite mass of the body, as you can see in the following drawing freely adapted from Oskar Schlemmer.

The dancer reaches into space, radiating energy.

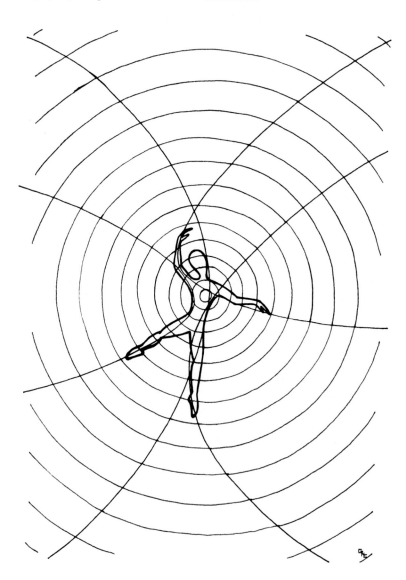

It is the goal of every teacher or ballet master to do the following:

Goals of the Ballet Class

1. Develop natural alignment potentials and efficient use of the body in motion founded upon each individual student's natural instrument. There is an unexplainable sensation of rightness and ease when the body moves from the standpoint of cardiovascular and muscular efficiency.
2. Instill a disciplined approach to physical and mental performance.
3. Transmit the best traditions of the past generations of teachers and dancers, such as the delicacy of true style—the rhythmic and dynamic shading inherent in each step.
4. Establish positive attitudes about classical dance but, most importantly, about your "self." Increased awareness and understanding of your own artistic, creative, and physical potentials are intrinsic to the dance experience. The teacher brings to the lesson an experienced awareness and judgment along with an objectivity from which each student can be nurtured and challenged.
5. Introduce technique in a progressive and appropriate manner in accordance with the physical and mental development of the class.

Important is the quest for the ideal, the ultimate. Writers like Edwin Denby have set before us the goal of perfection. "The expressive meaning is divided between recognizable details and the visual grace . . . the consistency is as if the most usual and easy ballet steps set a pitch for the eye—a pitch of carriage and balance in action . . . the overall effect is that of a spontaneous harmony of action."[3]

True dance is a response from feeling deep within oneself. Retired New York City Ballet ballerina, Melissa Hayden, was emphatic in stating that in order to develop a role, regardless of whether it was abstract or dramatic, she had to be able "to ground every action on stage to a reality of feeling" somewhere in experience.[4]

For a teacher, there is no feeling of satisfaction like experiencing those times when dancers exhibit "a new side of themselves, the beginning of an awareness of line, something emerging emotionally that you can encourage, guide."[5]

This all sounds so serious, yet there is a joyousness of spirit and fun which accompanies the unquenchable sense of accomplishment you are going to experience.

And now, off to class. . . .

Dressing for the Dance

Your teacher will provide a list of shops which sell shoes, leotards, and tights—the proper attire for dancing. The exact color may or may not be stipulated by your teacher. Usually, men will purchase tights listed as men's since they have been cut especially for the male physique and are heavier in weight. The colors available for men are more limited than for women.

Be sure to try on tights in the store, or read carefully the size charts provided by each manufacturer. Considered to be an undergarment, tights are not returnable. Purchasing the wrong size can be an expensive error.

Equal care should be given to the purchase of your ballet shoes, nearly handmade slippers constructed of elk skin or canvas. Follow your teacher's advice closely. Be on the safe side and have the shoes checked by your instructor before wearing them. Again, once the shoes have been worn, they cannot be returned. The shoe will feel very tight! (You must keep toe nails clipped short and straight across the toes.) There are two reasons for this necessity:

1. If there is shoe space beyond the toes, the shoe will not conform clearly to the foot when it is pointed, and the beauty of your footwork will be muffled.
2. Should the shoe not move in absolute precision with the foot, a dancer is more likely to lose balance or become injured when landing from a leap or when executing a spin on one foot.

You will, in a short time, become accustomed to this close-fitting shoe. Do not purchase ballet shoes in the late afternoon when your feet are more swollen than in the morning. Men usually purchase black or white shoes, while women generally wear pink, white, or black. Again, your instructor may have a preference.

Woman's Costume. Traditionally women wear pink tights and pink or black leotards. But now that an almost infinite spectrum of colors and range of styles exist, it is best to consult your instructor prior to purchase. If colored tights are permitted, get them the same color as the leotard or in an harmonious tone.

Since the body image you project should not be discordant but instead unified, wear tights *under* the leotard. Although panties are not generally worn under the tights, they can be if you feel more comfortable. A bra should be worn to protect the fragile tissues and to enhance aesthetic lines. Hair, if long, must be secured off the back of the neck and away from the face. Excessive jewelry must be avoided both for safety and aesthetic reasons. Dancing in pointe shoes, though an important part of classical dance, is not introduced until at least the intermediate level. So rigorous is it on the body, a dancer must train consistently for a minimum of one year before she is fully ready to dance *sur les pointes*.

Man's Costume. A dance belt, a kind of an athletic supporter, is worn to prevent hernias and to improve the aesthetic line. Like any elasticized garment, the feeling of restraint will not be entirely comfortable at first wearing. It is worn under the tights. Either a man's leotard or a tight-fitting cotton T shirt is worn over the dance belt. The shirt edges can be tucked into it to keep the shirt smooth as you move during class. Then the tights are put on and pulled up as high as possible, beyond the waistline so that the tights do not bag at the crotch. To hold the tights in place, a belt can be worn or suspenders attached.

A Final Word. Regular showering and use of a deodorant is an absolute necessity. Odors seem to adhere to synthetic fibers more readily than to natural. Following each lesson the dance costume should be washed in cold water and hung out to dry, or tumble dried at a cool temperature setting. Once body odor permeates the fibers, removing stale odor is much more difficult.

Leg warmers, woolly-knit tights similar in purpose to sweat pants, can help the critical muscles in the lower back, thighs, and calves to retain heat during the waiting periods between each exercise or combination. Whether they are truly necessary depends upon the intensity of the classwork, temperature of the studio, and whether drafts are a problem. A light, tight-fitting sweater might also be advised during the winter months or in extreme air conditioning.

Dancers who, either because of personal need or the combined heat and humidity of the studio, sweat profusely are advised to bring a small terry cloth towel to class. Drop the towel over the barre or fold it neatly on the floor where you are standing. Forehead sweatbands are also in common use, especially by men.

The Protocol of Taking Class

Every activity of life has its unwritten rules. To outsiders, they are a mystery, but to insiders, they are a comforting structure. Taking a ballet class will be easier once you are comfortable with its special rules of organization. You will then be able to anticipate the next activity and be better able to balance your expenditure of mental and physical effort throughout each lesson.

Before class begins, prepare yourself by limbering the body to reduce mental cares as well as joint stiffness. (See Chapter 2.) In addition, the class may begin with a few more conditioning rather than balletic exercises as a *pre-barre*.

The first 1/3 to 1/2 of the class will be spent performing exacting exercises while holding on to the *barre,* that hand-railing affixed to the walls of the studio. Since its function is to assist good alignment, while your energies are focused on the execution of movement with the leg and side of the body farthest away from the barre, proper hand grip is imperative. The hand should rest easily on top of the barre, thumb in line with the fingers instead of gripping it like a vice.

Hand A, with thumb in line with fingers, illustrates correct barre grip; Hand B, with hand encircling the barre, illustrates incorrect barre grip. (Source: author)

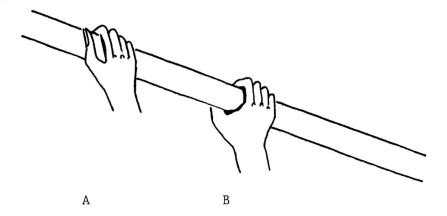

A   B

How far away from the barre should you stand? Extend the arm fully (forward if facing the barre or sideward if the body is parallel to it), rotate the elbow outward so that the joint bends slightly. Then, place the hand on the barre. Never grip the barre as though your hand was a "C" clamp. Instead, lay the hand closest to the barre over the top with the thumb in line with your fingers.

Dancer stands correct distance from barre. The inside arm approximates 2nd position with the hand placed on the barre slightly in front of the body.

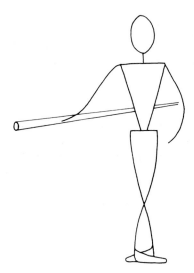

Do not allow the elbow to droop toward the floor. You are standing too close to the barre if the elbow must bend to an extreme angle. This also destroys the lifted, open carriage of your torso.

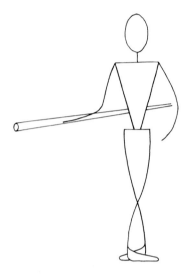

Dancer is standing too close to the barre.

Although the primary movements comprising the barre work will differ from teacher to teacher, the following list includes most of those you will learn during the first year of training: *plié, battement tendu, battement glissé, battement degagé, rond de jambe à terre, battement fondu, battement frappé, petit battement, relevé, grand battement, battement développé, cambré,* and *port de bras.* A complete definition and description of each, along with pointers for good execution, illustrations, and further variations are given in later chapters. Different combinations of these steps set to a variety of short musical selections will be designed by your teacher.

Remembering our definition of ballet, which includes the harmonious, perfected order, and geometry of absolute body lines, the need for precise positions of head, body, arms, feet, and directions to face become clear. Instead of stultifying the dancer into dry, almost boring shapes, these limitations actually free the dancer. The body's trajectory, its ultimate potential for line and design, is fully revealed. The dancer is "in balance."

The Language of Classical Line

The small square of space in which each dancer is contained is the structure for the clean linearity which comprises each and every movement in the classical vocabulary.

Remove the dancer for a moment. Replace the figure with a vertical line to represent the invisible line of gravity around which all the biomechanical forces generate and form when the body achieves balance and motion. Each corner of the box is joined by an invisible line of energy and focus. The arms and legs, amplified by specific head positions and a slight tilting of the shoulders and upper torso, extend outward form the center core of the body along these diagonal paths.

The dancer moves within an invisible box through which the lines and shapes which are created extend into space.

With the dancer removed, the line of gravity, around which the dancer centers his energy, is fully exposed.

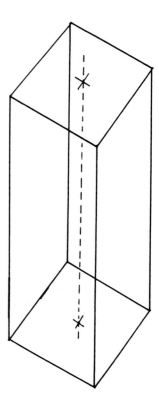

Besides extending and then initiating movements on diagonals, the body uses forward, backward, and sideward directions as well. Viewed from overhead, these diagonals and straight lines are joined in a simple floor pattern to which the early 20th century ballet master, Enrico Cecchetti, set a pattern of numbering still used by many teachers to simplify facing direction instructions.

For orientation to the stage, teachers may also use theater designations by referring to the front of the room as *downstage,* the right wall as *stage right,* the back wall as *upstage,* and the left wall as *stage left.* Therefore, in the following illustration, downstage and #5 refer to the front of your classroom, the wall you face when dancing in the center.

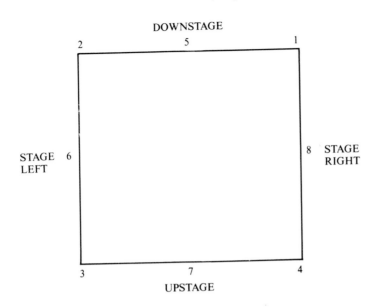

DOWNSTAGE

STAGE LEFT

STAGE RIGHT

UPSTAGE

The imaginary stage space the dancer uses as numbered by Enrico Cecchetti with standard theater stage directions.

Diann depicts the basic body positions which are based upon the diagonal and flat spatial lines used in classical dancing. Practice the positions diligently in front of a mirror until they begin to be comfortable to you. (Although you are wearing soft ballet slippers, seeing Diann in pointe shoes should give you a better sense of how the lines of the body are elongated in classical dancing.)

Croisé devant.

Effacé devant.

À la quatrième devant.

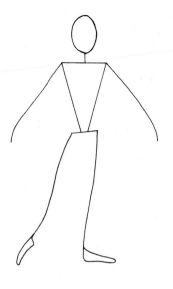

Pointe tendue à la seconde.   Éffacé derrière.

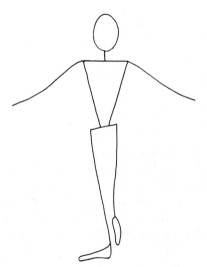

À la quatrième derrière.   Croisé derrière.

The next phase of the lesson occurs in the center of the studio, facing the mirrors should your studio have them. Since the initial orientation of court performances was to dance in honor of the king, the first theaters were designed as a picture frame, called a proscenium. The dancers were set off as jewels in this setting. So do we today in our earliest classes learn to face a specific front, as though performing on a proscenium stage with the audience seated just beyond the walls you face. Because of this performing situation, the designs and shapes of classical ballet are very specific and focused.

Center Practice

Many of the barre exercise movements will be repeated in the center, first alone, and then in combination with other movements, which will promote a stronger sense of dancing. See the two chapters concerning the vocabulary of center work. The kinds of movements to be learned in the center include: *sauté*—to jump, *jeté*—to leap, *temps levé*— to hop; *chassé*— to slide, *tourné*—to turn, a variety of *pas*—specific step patterns, and finally, *rèvèrence*— the slow, courtly bow to end class.

Varying the quality and tempo of the music, performing movements in a series on a diagonal or across the room, executing slow, controlled, axial movements, or a series of quick locomotor actions, varying direction, dynamics, and style are some of the ways in which your instructor will color these primary movements. Each sequence you learn will then take on special meaning and be a unique challenge.

Learn to use the full space of the studio and develop a sense of "playing" with your imagined audience, performing for enjoyment while you move. As you learn various sequences, memorize the arm and head positions as well. Too often, students think of these body parts as details to be learned at some later date. In reality the ease and ultimate perfection of a movement is frequently entirely dependent upon a careful manipulation of the forces of gravity and inertia. An improper tilt of the head or uncontrolled flailing of the arms could spell disaster to an otherwise conscientious effort.

Musical Accompaniment

No introduction to ballet protocol could be complete without some mention of the basis upon which dance rests, music. Early dance teachers composed ballet dancing to the singing quality heard during violin solos and in operatic arias. The music selected for your class will be simply structured, usually duple or triple meters (2/4, 4/4, 3/4, 6/4, or 6/8). The phrasing of the combinations is almost entirely a multiple of 8, 16, or 32. This can be either counts or measures. Yet, within this seeming simplicity is an almost infinite variety of colorations, from lyric to percussive, quick to slow, light to heavy.

For variety and interest, jazz, soft rock, and classical music can be excellent accompaniment. But you should begin by recognizing that the strong melodic lines, clear rhythmic foundations, defined accents, chord structure, and the variety of dynamics and emotional feeling embodied in the musical literature from the Romantic era are best suited to the ballet. Selections by such composers as Carl Czerny, Frederic Chopin, Johannes Brahms, Johan Strauss, P. I. Tchaikovsky, Leo Delibes, and Ludwig Minkus will probably constitute the heart of the music chosen for your classes. Their music instills the proper principles of moving through space. In ballet, this relationship is unique, resulting in an harmonious visualization of the underlying structure of the music and a positive dancer-musician relationship.

To increase your ear training as you learn the combinations, listen first to the meter; count it in multiples of 3 or 4. Try to be fully aware of accent, tempo, and quality. Relate these properties directly to the movements. Let the music "tell" you how to do the movements, then coordinate the movement to the music. Develop accuracy in counting so that you perform the sequence consistently regardless of how fast or slow the music is.

At the beginning of an exercise or center combination, the accompanist will play a few chords or measures as an introduction. Frequently, you will perform some kind of arm pattern (port de bras) in order to prepare for moving. Take a deep breath and exhale in time to the music. Release extraneous neck and shoulder tension while mentally sensing the first movements to be performed.

In this chapter you have been introduced to some of the mysteries of the dance studio. Begin practicing the poses in front of a mirror so that your body becomes used to them. Develop your ear to the music frequently used in the ballet class by listening to dance music from the great ballets, such as Delibes' *Coppelia,* or Tchaikovsky's *Swan Lake.* Move with the music, letting its changes in intensity alter your own mood.

See you in class. . . .

Study Questions

1. What are the properties which make ballet what it is?
2. What do you feel are the two most important goals a ballet teacher attempts to achieve in classwork?
3. What are the differences between the way a ballet shoe and a street shoe should fit?
4. What usually occurs during the first phase of the lesson?
5. For what purposes is a *barre* used in class?
6. Name three exercises usually included in the *barre* exercises.
7. Name the facing directions used in ballet.
8. Complete this floor pattern figure devised by Enrico Cecchetti.

downstage
upstage

9. How is music used in the ballet class?

1. Jean Georges Noverre, *Letters on Dancing and Ballets,* trans. Cyril Beaumont, **End Notes**
   (orig. 1803, New York: Dance Horizons, Reprint, 1966), p. 1.
2. Carlo Blasis, *The Code of Terpsichore,* trans. R. Barton (orig. 1831, New York:
   Dance Horizons Reprint, n.d.), p. 159.
3. Edwin Denby, *Dancers, Buildings and People on the Streets,* (New York: Curtis
   Books, 1965), p. 141.
4. Melissa Hayden, *Melissa Hayden, Off Stage and On,* (Garden City: Doubleday
   & Co., 1963), p. 93.
5. Marian Horosko, "Woytek Lowski," *Dancemagazine,* April, 1983, p. 82.

Port de bras practice begins at the barre. Texas Christian University. (Linda Kaye, photographer)

Preparing for Your Lesson

2

Getting ready to take a dance lesson is one of the most important aspects of studying dance. All too frequently students rush into the studio just moments before the opening measures of music. Without having given both the body and mind time to focus upon what is about to take place, the dancer is not really ready to begin. Efficiency of learning is lessened if a student is still brushing away thoughts of a previous activity while simultaneously trying to develop the finely-tuned body and mind necessary in the training of a ballet dancer.

Ideally, the student should review the previous lesson at home by mentally performing movements and step combinations. Mental rehearsals will aid the process of learning terminology and memorizing steps. That we actually can, through a visualization of our body in performance of poses, movements, and patterns in our mind, train nerve and muscle responses has been proven to be beneficial in learning complex body responses. Ballet is just such an activity. Devote a few minutes each day—in bed before retiring, on a bus, in line at the bank—mentally seeing yourself perform such movements as plié or rond de jambe remembering your instructor's comments on your or the class's performance. Practice what you will read in this book about the correct execution of each step. Quite quickly, as you discipline yourself to follow through with this important self-learning device, your body will begin to respond in a way that will make it seem as though it is learning the steps almost by itself. Your ability to remember the steps, what you have read, and what your instructor has said will also improve. This facet of learning is vital. The *mental knowing* spells success in the study of dance.

Warming Up

The second step in preparing for class is one which the beginner frequently overlooks but the advanced dancer never does. Physically preparing the body for a muscularly and cardiovascularly demanding activity is important. Joint and muscle discomfort following a work-out can be minimized while improvement in the ability of the body to respond most effectively during the class can be noticed if a short warm-up period precedes the lesson.

It must be remembered that the order of the barre and the primary movements like plié, battement tendu, and rond de jambe are as much traditional as physiological. Each action at the barre demands a mental as well as a physical, isolated focusing of the body's energies in terms of accepted fitness factors: strength, endurance, and flexibility. Therefore, most dancers come to the studio 10 to 15 minutes early in order to *warm-up* and spend a little time practicing poses or reviewing difficult movements from the previous lesson.

Raising the temperature of the body, increasing the blood supply, limbering the major joint areas used in dancing as well as releasing muscular tension are among the accepted benefits of a warm-up period.

Additionally, the student can devote a few minutes to exercise some areas of the body which are not specifically developed at the beginner level. For example, strength of the abdominal wall is vital to the efficient use of the body. Yet, because so much class time will be devoted to introducing ballet vocabulary, the abdominal area may be short-changed. The student must develop and maintain abdominal strength.

Strength of the back and of the arms must also be developed by the student. In ballet, the arms are used in an aesthetic, pictorial way and as a counter balance to enhance momentum or to change direction. But, in order for the body to operate efficiently, strength, endurance, and flexibility cannot be developed in only one half of the body. The student, therefore, must work to increase arm and shoulder girdle strength since the lower back, hips, legs, and feet are emphasized in ballet technique.

Frequently a beginner will discover that old postural habits must be reordered, replaced by new, more positive aesthetic and efficient alignment concepts. The process of scraping away old methods of perceiving and moving is a long-term project.

Each one of us has unique problem areas in the body. Perhaps your feet are stiff; you have difficulty in holding your legs in turned out positions; or the backs of your thighs are overly tight. Whereas the technique lesson is generalized in that everyone in the class performs the same movements, your warm-up routine should consist of those activities you need in order to prepare for the lesson. Such factors as weather, the status of your mental and physical health, the length of time since the previous lesson, and extraneous tension or fatigue may very well alter the kinds of actions the body needs to achieve optimum performance levels. Keep your regimen flexible, adjusting it to meet your mental and physical needs.

Nourish your body by selecting movements from the seven basic body zones developed in the dance lesson: aligning body parts, limbering the lower spine, increasing abdominal strength, increasing foot and ankle articulations, limbering the upper spine and shoulder girdle, practicing turn out of the legs, and increasing hip flexibility.

The exercises described are examples and illustrations of typical exercises from the listed categories; feel free to substitute other similar exercises. Select one or two movements from each category in order to devise a personal routine which is at least 10 minutes in length, yet not longer than 15–20 minutes. Warming up should do just that. Do not exhaust yourself. Record the exercises on a chart provided at the end of this chapter, then time each of the seven categories to insure that you are devoting a sufficient amount of time to each one. Following are illustrated descriptions of exercises. Try them all before deciding what to include in your personal warm-up.

The Warm-up Routine

Arts Magnet High School of Dallas finalist and others competing in the ARTS Recognition and Talent Search in Miami, Florida.

Samples of Warm-up Activities

Alignment of Thigh, Pelvis, and Spine

Thigh lifts with straight knee in supine hook lying position.

1. Lie on back, with knees bent, feet flat on the floor, arms down at your sides: Bend the R knee into your chest without allowing alignment of the pelvis to change. Extend R leg toward ceiling and lower to floor. Recover foot to original position. 8 times; repeat with L leg.
   Note: Keep neck and shoulders relaxed. Do not arch back or lift pelvis from the floor.

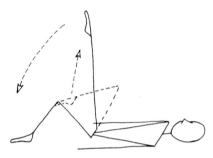

2. Same position as exercise 1: curl pelvis under and push it up toward ceiling without lifting heels from floor or arching the lower back. Lower slowly to floor beginning with upper back, keeping pelvis off the floor as long as possible and curling the spine. 6 times.
   Note: Sense being pulled up to the ceiling by hooks attached to the pelvic bones. Peel the pelvis off the floor.

Hip thrusts in supine hook lying position.

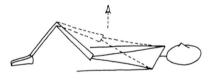

Limbering the Lower Spine

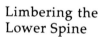

1. Sit very straight with the soles of the feet touching and spaced a comfortable distance from the pelvis; hold the feet with both hands: Allow the weight of the head to bend your torso forward without tilting the pelvis. Gently pulse in this position 16 times, then return to starting position. Change the R hand resting the palm on the floor near the hips and put the L hand in 5th position en haut. Allow the weight of the head to pull the entire torso into a right sideward curve. Pulse in this position 8 times, then return to original position. Circle torso forward and around to L side.
   Note: Do not allow waistline on the deeply curved side to collapse or the shoulders to lift.

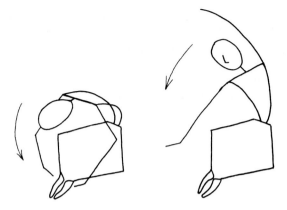

Spine pulses in the butterfly position.

2. Stand facing away from the barre with waist almost touching it, place hands on the barre as illustrated: Maintain an erect spine while bending forward at the hips as far as you can go. Allow spine to curve until the torso is hanging from the hips. Do not allow the knees to bend. Curl the torso back up to an erect position. 4–6 times.
   Note: Let head and neck relax at the depth of the forward hang.

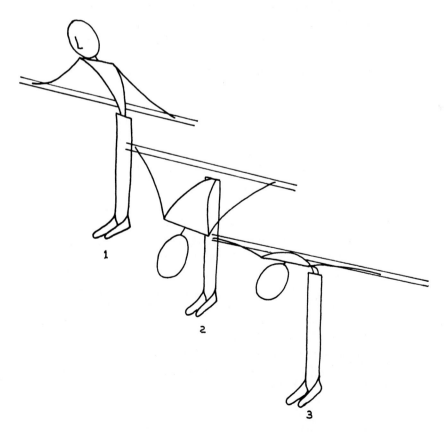

Slow body waves standing facing away from the barre.

3. Face the barre with waist almost touching it, feet together; place hands on barre approximating 2nd position: Without allowing hips to tilt, curve head and upper spine forward as far as possible. This will be a small movement. Return spine to original position. Then, again beginning with head, bend slightly backward by lifting chin toward ceiling. Do not involve lower spine. 4 times. Repeat adding a small plié during the forward curve action.

Upper back bending. Stand with waist close to the barre.

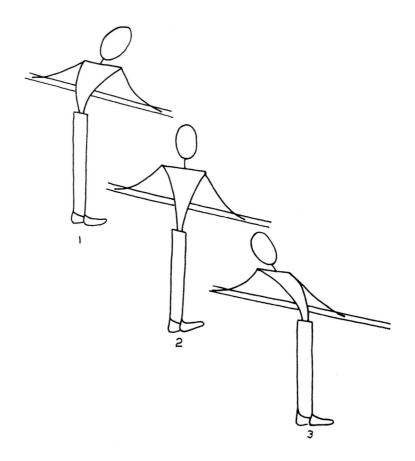

Increasing Abdominal Strength

1. Lie on back with knees bent and feet flat on floor, hands clasped behind the head as shown: Curve torso and head half-way up to seated position. You should not end in an erect position but maintain a curved spine. Hold position for 4 counts. Roll sequentially down to floor. Begin with 6 curl sit-ups and gradually increase to 22.
Note: Sense yourself curling around a tire or donut.

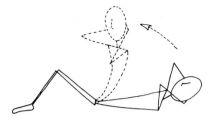

Curl sit-ups in a hook position. Remember to lift the head first.

2. Lie on back with legs fully extended overhead at an angle; legs are turned out in ballet 5th position. Notice that arms are straight next to the hips and act as a counter balance. Do 16 changement. Bring knees to chest to rest. Extend legs again and repeat 16 changement. Work up to 4 sets.
   Note: Waistline must remain pressed downward into the floor.

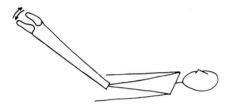

Changements in supine lying position. Keep waistline firmly on the floor. As abdominals strengthen, lower the level of the legs.

3. Lie on back with knees pulled to chest: Hug knees and pick head up to rock back and forth. 8 times. Lower back and head to floor. Rest and repeat.
   Note: Feel a strong curving action in pelvic area while maintaining a tight hug.

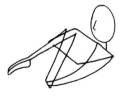

Rocking horse in supine position. Keep head tucked between knees.

1. Sitting on the floor, remove ballet shoes: Flex toes off the floor. Roll toes one at a time down to floor. Alternate beginning with little and great toe. Do 4 sets of alternating "piano rolls" with each

Articulating Feet and Ankles

foot. Work up to 8 sets with each foot.

Note: Keep arch and ankle well lifted throughout.

"Piano rolls" in a seated position. Articulate each toe.

2. Either standing or sitting: (1) slowly extend the foot from a completely flexed position, (2) then extend only the long arch, and (3) extend the metatarsal area. Reverse these steps to end with foot in a flexed position. Flex-extend 8 times with each foot.

Note: Toes must remain in line with the ankle at all times.

Sequentially flex and extend (1) ankle, (2) instep, and (3) metatarsals and toes.

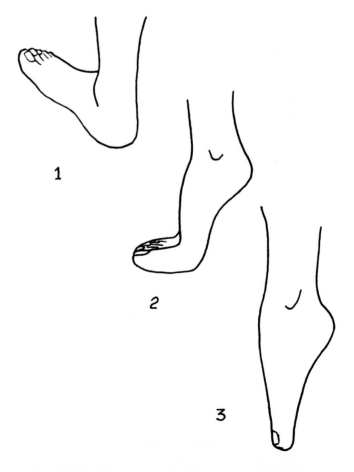

1

2

3

3. Stand facing the barre in 1st position with arms extended in 2nd
position and holding the barre as shown: Brush foot to 2nd position
and slowly circle the ankle 8 times outward and 8 times inward.
Close foot into 1st position, demi plié. Repeat with other foot.

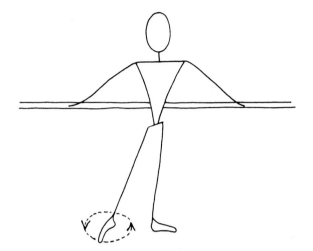

Standing foot circles in 1st
position.

4. Same position as above: Brush L foot until fully extended in 2nd
position. Lower the metatarsal area and then the heel. Do not
allow knees to bend; maintain turn out in both thighs. Pelvis will
tilt downward slightly toward the working side, but do not let it
droop. Return to point position making sure that the weight is
again centered over supporting leg. 4 times and close to 1st
position. Repeat with other leg. 2 times alternating sides.
Note: Press inner portion of ankle forward to increase use of the
upper thigh. Do not allow ankle or arches to roll as heel presses to
the floor.

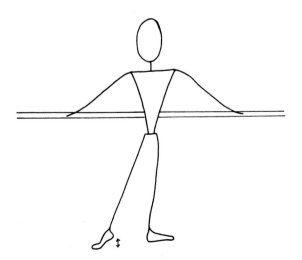

Standing metatarsals relevé
in pointe tendue position.

Limbering Arms
and Shoulders

1. Stand in an erect position: Make large backward circles with one arm without twisting the hips. Allow focus to follow the circling arm. 8 times with each arm, then make forward circles. Do actions simultaneously for a windmill effect.
   Note: Do not allow ribs to pop forward or shoulders to raise during circling action.

Backward arm circling. Try
not to twist in the hips.

2. Stand in an erect position, arms extended overhead: (1) reach strongly upward with the R arm focusing upward and allow R arm to relax slightly, (2) reach upward with L arm and then relax L arm. 8 times alternating arms.
   Note: Imagine that you are reaching straight up a tall chimney and can barely see the sky.

Standing overhead reaches.
Do not lift hips.

3. Stand erect and reach one arm directly overhead with elbow fully
   extended: Circle arm overhead beginning with small sized circles
   and gradually increase to involve upper spine. Focus slightly
   upward. Do not involve hips or let knees bend. Do circles with
   each arm; repeat with both arms together.
   Note: Elbows remain in line with the ears. Shoulders are relaxed.

Overhead arm circling.
Begin small and increase
the size of the circles.

1. Stand facing barre, feet about 6″ apart with hands placed on
   barre: Release heels slightly from floor and rotate heels together to
   end in 1st position. Release heels and rotate legs back to original
   position. Do not bend knees at any time. 8 times slowly.

   Note: Sense the thigh and calf working together as one unit.

Developing Turn Out

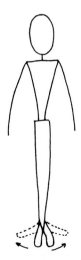

Rock weight onto heels and
turn out feet. Return weight
to a centered position.

2. Lie on back with legs extended, arms at sides, feet pointed:
(1) rotate legs outward. Do not disturb the extension of the feet or
lift waistline from floor, (2–3) hold turn out, (4) return legs to
original position. 20 thigh rotations.

Parallel to turned out leg
rotations in supine lying. Do
not let knees relax or ankles
twist.

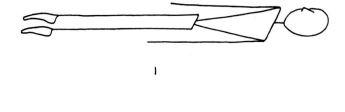

1

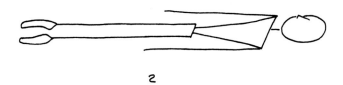

2

3. Stand facing barre foot extended to 2nd position with weight fully
balanced over supporting leg: Alternate rotating leg inward and
outward. Keep foot fully extended throughout. 10 times with each
leg.
Note: Do not allow pelvis or ribs to twist.

Standing leg rotations in
pointe tendue position.

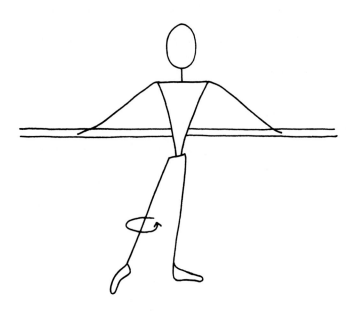

1. Stand as shown with R hand on the barre and feet in a comfortably turned out 1st position, arm in 2nd position: Swing L leg easily forward and backward brushing through 1st position between each set. Allow knee to bend as thigh is lifted. 16 times. Turn to face other direction and repeat with R leg.
   Note: Keep pelvis even and emphasize foot brushing fully as it passes through 1st position.

Increasing Hip Flexibility

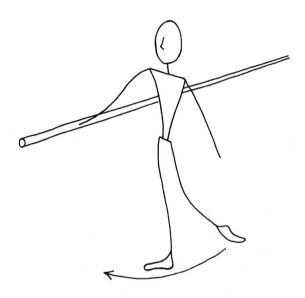

Easy leg swings through 1st position in a forward-back direction.

2. Lie on floor with R leg extended and L leg bent close to chest, arms grasping the bent knee: Slowly circle the L thigh in an outward circle. Hold abdominals tight to prevent motion in the pelvis. 6 times with each leg.
   Note: Press waistline into floor.

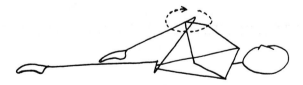

Thigh circling, keeping waistline pressed to the floor.

3. Face barre in a wide 2nd position with hands on barre as shown: Slowly bend the L knee making sure that it remains centered over the L foot. Beware of turning out too much. Deepen lunge without lifting L heel or displacing pelvis. Return to original position. Repeat with R leg. 8 times alternating sides.

Alternate leg lunges facing either towards the barre or away. Press the knee back over the instep of the foot.

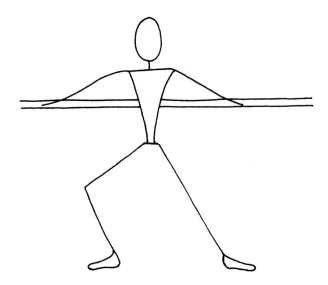

Now that you have tried each of these exercises, use the following chart to construct your own Personal Warm-Up Regimen. Make sure that at least one exercise is included for each of the seven basic body areas. Time your routine so that it is at least 10 minutes in length.

Personal Warm-up Routine Chart			
Category	**Exercises**	**Number of Repetitions**	**Time**
Alignment Practice			
Limbering Spine			
Abdominal Strength			
Foot and Ankle Articulation			
Arm and Shoulder Flexibility			
Turn Out Practice			
Hip Flexibility			
		Total Warm-Up Time	

Study Questions

1. What are some of the benefits of mentally rehearsing posture, steps, or movement sequences learned during the previous lesson?
2. What are the purposes for warming up in the studio a few minutes before the lesson begins?
3. Name the 3 primary physical fitness factors. Why are they critical in the training of a dancer?
4. How long should the pre-class warm-up last?
5. In order to fully prepare the body for a ballet class, basic body areas need to be exercised. Name them.
6. Why is it important for each dancer to devise an individualized warm-up routine?

Men's technique emphasizes spectacular jumps. Brigham Young University Theatre Ballet.

In rehearsal . . . Louisiana State University Ballet Ensemble. (Danny Fike, photographer)

Fundamental Theories of Ballet Technique

3

Although the student memorizes and practices many different body facings, poses, and steps, perfection in dance is achieved only to the degree that the student develops, remarked Asaf Messerer, the great Russian teacher at the Bolshoi, "beauty of line, the plastic design of the arms and body, the lightness of jump and flight, and the expressiveness and musicality of execution."[1]

The key ingredient tying these qualities into one concept is biomechanical economy. Each dancer strives to bring action of the body into accordance with the natural laws of motion and balance. The efficiency of movement, economy of effort, and lessening of unwanted muscle tension do not result from thoughtless repetition of the various exercises . . . No. These subconscious understandings come about gradually by relating the stylistic elements of dance to functional body physics.

One's first concern must be to compare present postural habits with those which kinesiologists have found to be the most efficient for the body.

Dance as the Harmonious Use of the Body

Muscles exist to move the skeleton, which then move the body through space. Other purposes exist, such as maintaining cardiovascular circulation and proper body temperature. But, let us focus only upon motion. Contraction, a controllable or automatic shortening of the muscle mass, changes the position of bones to which the muscles are attached. The movement is then colored by the amount of motion a specific joint structure permits. Let us explore two different joint structures. The hip, a ball and socket joint, allows the body to perform actions which differ from those of the elbow, a hinge joint.

Alignment— The Keystone to a Dancer's Technique

35

Move the thigh freely. Did you notice that it can move away from and toward the body, swing forward and backward, move in a circle as well as turn in and out? Now try the same movements with the elbow. Was it possible to do as many things with this joint? The elbow is limited to bending and straightening because of the nature of the joint structure.

As you take class, it will be important to guide your body through the exercises with a firm knowledge of the movement possibilities of each major joint area. Any attempt to move beyond the potential of a body part causes the rest of the body (in a chain reaction) to become misaligned in order to compensate. The result of faulty alignment is a gradual structural weakening of the joint or tiny tearing in adjoining muscle tissues. This eventually leads to an injury. Highly stylized though ballet may be, still its rules of balance, placement, and motion are based upon sound functional alignment.

Trained at the Paris Opera, Anna Paskevska writes: "Imposition of specific shapes on an unbalanced structure precludes ease of execution. Thus expression, characterization, and fluidity of motion are all beyond the range of dancers who have developed techniques that contradict their skeletal alignment."[2]

The following diagram illustrates the positive postural concepts dancers develop and maintain. Should you discover a postural fault, it will take more than your ballet class to overcome it. Take time periodically throughout the day to remind yourself to *pull up*. It is not really necessary to sense a restricting contraction of the superficial, surface muscles. Instead (1) sense your spine as a series of ABC blocks, each separated by a soft marshmallow. The blocks must be lifted, separating themselves from the marshmallows. Don't squash the marshmallows!

In addition, (2) press the back of the pelvis forward slightly, making sure that the whole torso moves forward with the pelvis to center your weight over the arches of the feet. (3) Lift the back of the waistline. (4) Lower your shoulders easily over the top of the rib cage. (5) Focus directly ahead; avoid looking at the ground when you walk.

Try these five simple reminders right now. Notice how much more energized, yet less tense and more alert, you feel. When the body is perfectly aligned, the surface muscles, those we commonly call clench, will feel slightly relaxed. The effort of maintaining the body in good vertical alignment will be transferred to the skeletal structure itself and maintained by the deep postural muscles, those closer to the bones and joints being manipulated.

*Diann demonstrates the
four reminders for good
posture.*

*Without innervating the
anti-gravity muscles, Diann
slouches with abdomen and
pelvis released, chin
forward, and chest sunken.*

When moving, the dancer fully applies all the alignment concepts learned during the static poses or exercises. The body's weight is held poised over the insteps so that the body is in dynamic repose, like a cat ready to leap. In order to preserve this readiness, the pelvis must remain over the insteps. Guard against these common postural errors: hyperextending the lower back and letting the weight of the pelvis drop back into the heels. The placement of the center of weight (situated lower in women then in men) is the key to controlling the body; misplacement of the pelvis can disrupt the center of weight. Both dynamic and static balance will be affected.

Since the pelvis absorbs weight, supports the lower part of the torso when the legs are being moved, and controls the center of gravity, it is imperative that the hips be maintained in an even, centered position. The entire spine, culminating with the head, is supported from the pelvis. Think of the pelvis, suggested Lulu Swigard, as though it is a bucket filled to the brim with water. Tilt it ever so slightly and the water will spill out. In a chain reaction, segments of the spine will compensate with adverse effects.

**The Body — A
Vehicle for
Motion**

Good posture begins with alignment of the pelvis, sensed as a bucket full of water, connecting the dancer from the floor to the top of the head. Lengthen spine fully.

Turn Out. Standing and moving the body with feet turned out is one of the primary components of classical dance and integral to the total alignment of the dancer's body. Exposing the attractive profile of the leg and arched foot emphasizes the aesthetic contours of the body. Many balletic step patterns consist of delicate, articulate leg gestures seen best when the legs are turned outward.

Beyond imparting a sense of beauty, turn out is also a valuable tool to facilitate the control of the body in space. A unified use of the body, in which the shoulders and hips move in concert, improves agility. Control and support for the pelvic floor and lower back are enhanced by strengthening the deep rotator muscles. The control of the upper thigh, pelvis, and lower back flows downward to provide support for the ankles and arches. Improved ability to balance over the supporting leg during slow adagio movements results.

To find your own natural turn out range, stand perfectly straight with your feet 6″ apart, facing forward. Place your hands just below the top of the pelvis, fingers extended diagonally downward. This will allow you to feel the activity in the hip joint as it rotates.

Rock slightly back onto your heels, and turn your feet outward as far as they can go. Do not squiggle your feet to increase the turn out. Rock back onto the whole foot. . . . This Is Your Turn Out Range. If the dancer is an adult, the hip joint structures are fully developed and ossified. Therefore, turn out cannot be increased beyond what the dancer has right now.

Nevertheless, a feeling of turn out will increase as the deep rotator muscles become stronger, better able to maintain your natural range during movement. The worst thing you could do is to pretend that you have more turn out by relaxing the knees, dropping or rolling the arches, or twisting the pelvis. All three common errors will decrease your ability to control the body during motion. Unnecessary stretching of critical foot and knee ligaments will be the actual and unwanted outcome.

The Feet. The foot, with its two major structural arches—the metatarsal and the longitudinal, is a marvelously engineered suspension bridge. The weight of the body must be balanced over three areas for greatest structural efficiency: the heel and the two tarsal joints located behind the first and fifth toes. The toes remain stretched, each pressing into the floor without curling. As the foot extends through the two arches to a full extension, the toes stretch without curling.

The foot flexes and extends with the ankle joint acting as a pivot. It must remain perfectly aligned to the calf when the foot extends. While standing, sense a strong upward lift under the longitudinal arch to prevent the ankle from rolling inward and thereby losing correct biomechanical functioning.

Body Signals. The body will transmit subtle signals when it is not being used in accordance with its own internal biomechanical standards. And a word of caution: never force your body instrument beyond its ability to maintain positions or shapes with unnecessary tension. Beware of the following inappropriate feelings:

> pressure in knee joints
> fatigue and discomfort in lower back
> inability to maintain lifted arches and ankles during plié
> a vice-like sensation in the buttocks in order to maintain turn out
> failure to bend the knees fully during jumps and leaps
> excessive tightness at the back of the neck
> flaccid thighs
> moving the pelvis uncontrollably
> constant hypertension between shoulder blades and in lower back
> tightness in chest during inhalation
> discomfort in the big toe joint
> burning sensation in knees and ankles

The five positions of the feet were stipulated over 200 years ago. Although predicated upon an absolute 180° turn out, even then one could modify the designs according to the potential of one's own turn out.

Fundamentals of Ballet Posture — Feet, Arms, Breath

Coordinated to these foot positions are complementary arm positions. These positions should be memorized immediately.

Feet—1st position, arms—1st position en avant (all positions according to the French school).

Feet—2nd position, arms—2nd position.

3rd position—feet and arms.

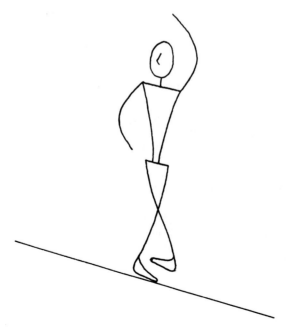

4th position—feet and arms.

Feet—5th position, arms—5th position en haut.

Be aware that the arms and hands are carried slightly forward of the spine, or line of gravity. When the arms are in 2nd position, they appear visually as though they are extended sideward. However, in reality the arms are extended on a slight forward angle as is seen in the overhead perspective. And in 5th position en haut, the hands are held slightly in front of the crown of the head.

Overhead view of dancer with arms in 2nd position. The arms curve naturally forward.

These basic arm and foot positions are in use constantly throughout all purely classical movements and designs. They become as road maps, those almost automatic laser sharp signals or reference points, informing the muscle receptors and the central nervous system that the patterns are being performed correctly. Then either balanced stillness or motion will be achieved successfully.

Not only do the arms create clean architectural lines, augmenting the design of the torso, legs, and feet, but they provide an attractive picture frame for the upper body and head. Their proper use will make your expenditure of effort/energy more effective.

The architectural and flow lines created when a dancer's leg extends to 2nd position with 3rd position en haut arms.

The timing and position of the arms can improve the efficiency of motion in relation to the functioning of the skeletal and muscular systems. Think of how important the accuracy is in the use of the arms for thrust, counter-balance, momentum, flow, etc., to a gymnast or a runner. Certainly the use of the arms in ballet is neither as complex a mechanism as in gymnastics nor as simple as in running. Your learning of the exact shapes used with certain movements or poses will make *the* difference between ease of movement and a constant battle against instability and awkwardness. The goal of the dancer is to move in balance. Many of the steps you will learn have standard arm patterns which are used whenever that step is performed.

While practicing the various arm patterns, notice that they usually begin or pass through en bas and first position en avant. This particular progression of the arms directs the body weight forward and slightly upward over the front part of the foot and on into space. At the same time, lifting the arm gives an appearance of generosity, volume, and lightness to movements.

Breathe deeply. Do you notice the chest lifting and lowering? Do you feel lighter on your feet during inhalation? Pretend that the upper arm is part of the rib cage. Allow the arm to levitate, rising slightly to the side when inhaling and floating back down when exhaling. Repeat this action until you can do it without tensing the neck or allowing the back to arch.

You have just experienced the most fundamental principle of arm use in classical dance. Based upon the natural breath flow of the body are ballet port de bras. When the body rises, steps, springs, or jumps, the arms will tend to rise with the inhalation that the body will take naturally. During exhalation, the body and arms will settle, relaxing back to the earth.

Proper breathing creates a visual experience, a kinetic sense of life, through diaphragmatic use of the arms. The lift of the arms away from the chest cavity also promotes deep breathing, an important part of developing stamina. Never hold your breath; never breathe only in the neck and upper chest.

True, a dancer does not breathe from the lower abdomen. To do so would mean that the dancer would lose the vital muscular support of the abdominal area, that link to pelvis and lower back needed in order to articulate the movements of the legs and feet. Nevertheless, a dancer takes advantage of the back and whole rib cage to achieve maximum oxygen exchange with each breath.

Imagine your ribs and back to be an accordion, opening and lifting during inspiration, then dropping and closing during expiration.[3]

What has been learned are some fundamental concepts which you should keep uppermost in mind as you progress in your studies of ballet. A thoughtful application of the principles of turn out, port de bras, breath flow, as well as

Like an accordian, the rib cage lifts and widens during inhalation.

A dropping and closing sensation is felt during expiration.

proper alignment must augment your diligent practice of exercises and steps. You can then more fully appreciate how ballet dancing does follow the immutable laws of nature.

Study Questions

1. How does good alignment assist the dancer?
2. In what joint area does turn out occur? What is the purpose of turn out in classical dancing?
3. What is the function of the pelvis in aligned motion?
4. List 3 inappropriate body feelings which serve as warning signals to the dancer?
5. Draw the 5 positions of the feet:

1st	2nd	3rd	4th	5th

6. What are the purposes of the stylized arm positions and patterns in ballet dancing?
7. To what does the term "rhythmic breath flow" refer?
8. How does the dancer control breathing while dancing?

End Notes

1. Asaf Messerer, *Classes in Classical Ballet,* trans. Oleg Briansky, Garden City: Doubleday & Co., p. 26.
2. Anna Paskevska, *Both Sides of the Mirror: The Science and Art of Ballet,* New York: Dance Horizons, 1982, p. 36.
3. Lulu Sweigard, *Human Movement Potential, Its Ideokinetic Facilitation,* New York: Harper & Row, Publishers, 1974, p. 241.

Practicing passé. Texas Woman's University Dance Repertory Theatre. (Jennifer Collins, photographer)

The Basic Barre

4

The traditional manner for beginning every ballet class is at the barre, that specially designed railing which stands approximately 40 inches from the floor. No matter how advanced the dancer, class always begins with a series of exercises practiced with the gentle aid of the barre. Ballet technique, with its emphasis on the use of the legs in a turned out manner, is not a natural use of the body. Consequently, muscle tonus and the ability to use a turned out leg must be re-established by all dancers at the beginning of each lesson.

When facing the barre, placement of the hands should approximate 1st position en avant, and 2nd position when the dancer faces parallel to it. Refer to chapter one for an illustrated explanation of the proper hand position on the barre. In order to develop the ability to remain centered over your supporting leg, stand neither too close nor too far away from the barre and remember never to grip the barre as though your hand were a "C" clamp.

Now you are ready to begin. . . .

Since every teacher assembles the exercises comprising barre practice in a slightly different order, in a format which may be altered as your class progresses, the following two chapters are organized as a source book. The most elementary movements of barre practice—those with which you will become immediately familiar—are presented in this chapter. Depending on how rapidly your class advances, your instructor will add additional movements. When this occurs, go on to study the next chapter. The concepts, rules of movement, and terminology are highly specific and complex. A number of movements, even in a book designed for the new dancer, may prove too difficult for you during this first year of work. Do not be discouraged. Every dancer, even the professional, has movements which always require extra thinking and effort to attain and maintain.

The purpose of barre practice is similar to the workout period in any sport. Strength, flexibility, and mental-muscular coordination will develop as you practice the primary components of every step in the classical vocabulary. For instance, the spectaular grand jeté en avant is a large forward leap in which both legs are stretched away from each other and the torso is fully extended. Broken into its various technical components, the grand jeté is a finely tuned coordination consisting of a bending preparation (plié), a high front kick (grand battement) to propel the body into the air, another kick (or battement) with the back leg extending behind the body (arabesque), and a recovery landing on one leg (fondu). These primary actions are first practiced and perfected during the various exercises at the barre before the dancer ever attempts a grand jeté as a step.

Leg bending—plié, body rising—relevé, straight leg beating—battement, and leg circling—rond de jambe constitute the family names for the fundamental movements along with torso bending—cambré which you will learn initially at the barre.

Qualities of movement will be varied, balanced, and progressively ordered from slow to quick, easy to difficult, and little strength to much strength. Muscularly easy and mentally simple actions are placed at the beginning of the lesson, while the more demanding movements are presented at the conclusion of the barre. The length of barre work varies from one teacher to another, but that section of your lesson usually lasts about half of the total length of the class. You should expect to be in a sweat and experience a sense of muscle fatigue, but not utter exhaustion, at the conclusion of this vital portion of the class.

The ballet steps you will learn in this chapter on basic barre exercises begin with demi and grand plié, elevé and relevé, battement tendu, battement tendu relevé, battement dégagé, battement développé, cambré, rond de jambe à terre, battement retiré, battement passé, grand battement and grand battement en clôche. Although these primary steps involving the legs have been disassociated from the port de bras (use of the head and arms), be reminded that all balletic motion, whether performed as part of barre practice or in the center, is a carefully coordinated effort of head, arms, torso, and legs. Fourth position of the feet is not recommended at the very beginning level since required for safe execution is control of the thighs, pelvis, and lower back. Reflecting this opinion, none of the movements described in this chapter use 4th position. Look upon this book as a resource, never as a replacement for concentrated class experiences.

The succeeding chapters on technique are organized so that each specific movement is defined to provide an understanding of the basic concept and the meaning of the French term. Memorize the correct pronunciation and begin to connect the name of the step with the action. How to execute the movement is explained, and specific reminders on good form for your performance of the step are listed. Covered also are errors that most dancers experience when doing that movement. Why the step is practiced, its value in terms of your overall physical development as a dancer, concludes the description and analysis of each step.

Demi Plié (de - MEE plee - AY)

Definition

A half bending of the knees which emphasizes the development of elasticity in the leg and flexibility in the ankle. Heels remain on the floor. Used as a preparation for most other movements, particularly jumps, steps, and turns. Performed in all foot positions.

Execution

Begin with both legs straight and turned out from the hip joint.

Sense a pressing outward of the inner part of the thigh before the body begins to lower.

Flex knees away from the center of the body maintaining knee alignment over the feet and retaining a strong vertical spine throughout.

Lower body until heels almost begin to rise from the floor.

Extend knees until dancer has returned to original position.

Demi plié in 2nd position.

Demi plié in 5th position.

1st position demi plié with incorrectly released pelvis.

Diann shows a number of alignment errors in demi plié: forward chin and shoulders, relaxed abdomen, tucked under pelvis, forward knees, and rolled forward back foot.

Reminders for Good Form

Maintain hips forward over the insteps.

Keep arches lifted and ankle bones aligned during the demi plié.

Sense the back of the thigh pressing forward throughout the plié; keep your weight centered over the legs.

Maintain torso and body weight evenly distributed over both feet.

Allow a smooth, continuous motion throughout the plié.

Keep spine fully extended.

Purposes

To learn correct alignment and use of the foot and leg sequentially while supporting the body's weight.

To develop leg and foot strength as well as elasticity.

To use thigh-hip rotator muscles.

To increase ankle, knee, and hip flexibility.

To practice maintaining extended torso alignment while lowering the body weight.

Grand Plié (grahn plee - AY)

Definition

A full bending of the knees until the thighs are parallel to the floor and the heels are released from the floor (except in 2nd position when the heels remain on the floor). Do in all positions of the feet, except 4th position which is difficult for the beginner to perform.

Execution

Begin with both legs straight and turned out.

Sense a pressing outward of the inner part of the thighs before the body begins to lower.

Once the knees have begun to bend outward (demi plié), allow them to continue opening to the sides until the legs can no longer bend without lifting the heels from the floor. Lower the body in a controlled manner.

Do not disturb the upright posture of the body.

Return to an erect posture, pushing downward against the floor and drawing the upper part of the inner thighs together.

 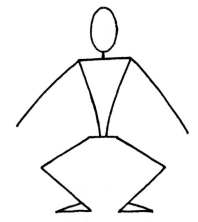

In grand plié in either 1st or 5th positions, the heels rise from the floor as a reaction to the deep opening of the thighs.

Do not release heels from the floor in grand plié in 2nd position. In all other positions, the heels do release.

Reminders for Good Form

Do not pause at any time during the grand plié.

Maintain upward support of the abdominal muscles and pelvic floor.

Keep oppositional stretch of the spine: upward vs. downward. Sense going up and down like a horse on the carousel.

Keep pelvis upright throughout the movement.

Open the thighs to the sides of the room rather than sensing only a lowering of the body. Fully apply demi plié reminders.

Maintain even support of the body weight through both feet. Maintain strong ankle-foot alignment by not rolling inward onto the big toe.

Press toes onto the floor without gripping the floor.

Let your own ankle and calf flexibility as well as thigh strength determine the depth of the grand plié.

Purposes

To strengthen thighs and lower pelvic support.

To develop strength and alignment of feet and ankles during full flexion of the ankle.

To strengthen turn out from the hips.

To practice postural alignment and develop back strength.

Elevé (el - e - VAY)

Definition

Rising on one or both feet to 3/4 pointe in a smooth, vertical motion.

Can be performed in all foot positions and extended leg poses.

Execution

Press heels upward as high as flexibility of ankles, insteps, and toes will permit. Keep knees extended.

Balancing in 1st position elevé. Florida School of the Arts, Prof. Christian Faust. (M. Wier, photographer)

Keep toes lying flat on the floor at all times. Do not "knuckle" the toes or contract them in an unnatural way.

Maintain the torso and hips so that the thrust of the rising action is directed through the invisible line of gravity which should bisect the hip, knee, and ankle joints.

Lower heels to the floor in a controlled manner; do not bend the knees or release the spine and pelvis from a vertical line.

Reminders for Good Form

Do not disrupt center of balance within the body.

Perfect smoothness during this action.

Allow the torso to ride high on top of hips throughout movement.

Sense a strong upward pressure from under the pelvis.

Allow the whole body to shift forward over the instep as the body rises to 3/4 pointe.

Time the full extension of the knee with lift of heels to insure a smooth, continuous rising action.

Purpose

To change the body's level in space in a vertical direction.

To practice coordinating extension of knees and ankles, while supporting the weight of the body.

Relevé   (ruhl - e - VAY)

Definition

A change in level to 3/4 pointe accomplished by a sharp spring upward while pulling the toes under the body's line of gravity. Used in movements, such as a sustained pose or pirouettes, where a shift of weight during the upward movement is not desirable. Performed in all foot positions and extended leg poses on one foot.

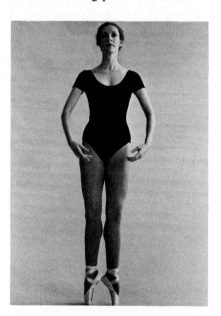

During a relevé, the toes scoop under the body to produce a vertical thrust.

Execution

Assume particular position and execute a quick demi-plié.

Spring directly up to 3/4 pointe by pushing off floor strongly while pulling toes in under the ankles.

Then, spring lightly off toes into a demi plié.

Reminders for Good Form

Remember to pull toes in under center of the body.

Maintain strong lift in waist so that the torso and pelvis remain in position.

Perform action with a strong, direct thrust without actually jumping or with any feeling of jerking up or down.

Time extension of knees with raising of heels for a smooth yet strong leg-foot action.

Purposes

Used as a preparation exercise for jumps and pirouettes.

Raises the dancer to 3/4 pointe in a strongly accented manner.

Develops strength in back, feet, and legs.

Develops coordination in the dancer, increasing the ability to move quickly.

Battement Tendu   (baht - MAHN tahn - DYOU)

Definition

A stretched beating of the leg in which the dancer has fully extended the leg and foot so that only the tips of the toes are touching the floor. Performed forward, sideward, and backward.

Execution

Begin in one of the closed positions of the feet.

Brush bottom of foot on the floor slowly outward until both arches of the foot lift and it is extended fully. Only the tips of the toes are touching the floor. This is called position *pointe tendue.*

Return to original closed position in reverse sequential order, first relaxing toes and ankle before drawing the working leg back to the beginning closed foot position.

Increase outward rotation of the leg as foot returns to position.

Center the body over both feet simultaneously with close of the working foot.

Reminders for Good Form

Neither knee bends at any time during the battement tendu.

Extend foot in sequential manner during the brushing movement, lifting the heel before allowing toes to extend.

Do not allow toes to "pop" off the floor.

Maintain turn out in working leg. Press ankle forward as foot extends.

At the finish of a battement tendu, the leg and foot are fully extended with no pelvic tilt.

Maintain good turn out in the supporting leg with the ankle and arch of that foot well lifted.

Maintain pelvic alignment without extraneous motion as leg is moving during the battement tendu.

Be sure to allow working foot to relax as it returns to original position, shifting weight back to both feet.

Purposes

Strengthens and increases elasticity of foot through the alternation of tension and relaxation.

Develops ability to use the leg in isolation from the torso.

Prepares dancer for any action which includes a straight leg extension.

Increases dancer's ability to balance on one leg while moving the other one.

Battement Tendu Relevé (baht - MAHN tahn - DYOU ruhl - e VAY)

Definition

A rising and lowering of the stretched leg beat. Usually performed to 2nd position.

Execution

Perform a battement tendu to 2nd position from either 1st or 5th position.

Lower toes only to the floor without allowing heel to lower or knee to flex. (Sometimes the whole foot is lowered.)

Extend toes fully and complete a tendu before returning to starting position.

Can be performed singly (as described) or in a series.

Reminders for Good Form

Maintain turn out on the supporting leg.

Do not relax abdomen or allow pelvis to tilt.

Toes will draw slightly back toward body center as they lower and move slightly away from body as foot returns to full pointe tendue.

Can be performed devant and derrière as well.

Purposes

Increases strength and flexibility in metatarsal area of foot.

Develops the ability to maintain outward thigh rotation for an extended duration.

Battement Dégagé   (baht - MAHN day - ga - ZHAY)

Definition

A disengaged stretched beating of the leg or a battement tendu which is allowed to rise about 4″ from the floor. It is performed in an accented manner. Also known as *battement jeté* (thrown) or *battement glissé* (glided).

Execution

Begin a battement tendu with a strong sense of pushing the foot into the floor. The foot brushes off the floor to the desired height and then returns to the original position.

Emphasize or accent the closing portion of this action.

Stretch toes through battement tendu before extending them off the floor in battement dégagé.

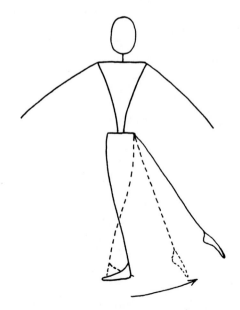

Reminders for Good Form

Do not allow the quick action of the leg to disturb alignment of the
torso and hips.

Lift lower abdominals throughout.

Sense a closing or drawing together of the groin or extreme top portion
of the inner thighs.

Use the foot sequentially, allowing it to relax somewhat as it brushes
the floor back into the starting position.

Transfer weight slightly back to two feet on the closing.

Practice the definite accent of this movement.

Purposes

Develops necessary strength and ballistic quality of leg and foot for
jumps.

Prepares the dancer to attempt higher extensions of the leg.

Develops the dancer's ability to control shifts in body weight during
motion without disrupting the supporting leg.

Strengthens muscles of inner thighs and feet.

Rond de Jambe à Terre en Dehors and en Dedans
(rohn duh ZHAMB a tair on deh - OR, on deh - DAHN)

Definition

Rotary action of the whole working leg in an outward or inward
direction. With the tips of the toes remaining in contact with the floor,
the leg inscribes a half circle. Usually music in 3/4 meter is played for
rond de jambe.

Execution

The dancer joins together pointe tendue devant - seconde - derrière
positions in a sequential arcing manner through 1st position.

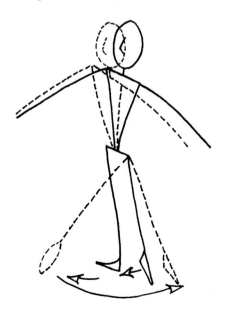

In an outside rond de jambe
(en dehors) connect pointe
tendue devant, seconde, and
derrière with a strong brush
through 1st position.

Either an inward *en dedans* (towards the center line of the body) direction is used or an outward one *en dehors* (away from the center line of the body).

Accent pointe tendue devant during en dehors and pointe tendue derrière during en dedans rond de jambe.

Reminders for Good Form

Maintain pelvis centered over supporting leg.

Do not allow supporting leg and foot to roll forward losing turn out in the thigh or dropping the arch.

Concentrate on opening thighs away from each other as rond de jambe progresses.

Do not put any weight on toes of working foot as it inscribes the circle.

Relax foot as it passes through 1st position, yet maintain a well-lifted arch.

Do not allow pelvis to twist in an attempt to increase turn out.

Purposes

Develops dancer's ability to coordinate moving the leg through a number of positions while simultaneously learning to compensate for the change in the center of gravity, and to maintain turn out of both legs.

Limbers the hip joints.

Prepares for more advanced movements such as *grand rond de jambe* and *pas de basque* which require the ability to perform this basic action.

Battement Retiré   (baht - MAHN ruh - tih - RAY)

Definition

A retracted or shortened leg beat performed from closed foot positions.

Execution

Draw working leg quickly up the supporting leg, toes maintaining contact with the calf of the supporting leg, to a position about 4″ below the knee cap in the front or directly under the belly of the calf muscle in the back.

Extend feet strongly throughout by pushing into the floor in order to retract the leg upward to position.

Retrace the working foot down the calf of the supporting leg, relaxing the foot only to return it to the beginning position.

Shift weight back to two feet smoothly as working foot lowers.

*Retiré devant, arm held in
1st position en avant.*

Retract the foot up to
position with a sense of
urgency.

Reminders for Good Form

Maintain a supported pelvis without any tilt.

Emphasize pushing the foot off the floor as opposed to lifting the thigh.

Maintain an extended working foot. Do not sickle or twist the foot as it
is drawn up or down the supporting leg.

As toes touch the floor, lower foot in sequential fashion to the floor (toe
- ball - heel) until weight shifts smoothly again to two feet.

Purposes

Increases balance by centering body's energy around line of gravity.

Develops dancer's ability to lift thigh while retaining turn out.

Passé (pah - SAY)

Definition

The action of passing. Begin and end in 5th position.

Execution

Perform a battement retiré. Continue past retiré position opening thigh
slightly until toes are touching the hollow of the supporting knee.

Lower thigh slightly as foot continues through battement retiré down
the back of the supporting leg to close in 5th position.

Reminders for Good Form

    Do not allow working foot to sickle or the supporting ankle to wobble.

    In order to maintain an even pelvis, the beginner will probably not be able to bring the foot to full height. That the pelvis remains level throughout is of utmost importance, so height of the passé should be varied accordingly.

The foot changes from front to back during a passé.

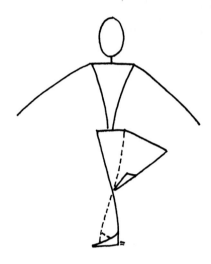

Purposes

    A primary transition for the working leg to change from front-to-back or back-to-front.

    A primary component of such movements as pas de chat, développé, and is frequently performed by itself combined with a relevé.

    Develops clear, articulate foot work.

    Increases strength and stability of pelvis, back, and thighs as preparation for extensions and pirouettes.

Développé   (dayv - loh - PAY)

Definition

    The unfolding of the working leg from the floor to a high extension.

    Performed devant, seconde, and derrière.

Execution

    Release working foot from a closed position and draw toes up side of supporting leg to passé position.

    Extend leg to desired height in a devant, seconde, and derrière position without allowing thigh to drop.

    Beginners will not extend to a pose higher than demi height (45°) in order to develop smoothness and control over both working and supporting legs.

Lower working leg carefully to pointe tendue then return to starting position.

Développé seconde. Line of the arm should complement that of the leg.

Reminders for Good Form

Once the height of the thigh is established, the lower leg must extend to that height. In other words, do not drop the level of the thigh as the lower leg completes the extension.

Do not allow the thigh of the supporting leg to turn inward or let that knee buckle during the développé.

Maintain the pelvis forward and upward over the supporting foot.

Perform at a smooth adagio tempo, punctuated with a slight hold of the fully extended position before lowering the leg to pointe tendue.

Keep the hips level yet allow some forward torso action when extending derrière to insure ease of balancing over supporting hip.

Purposes

A primary adagio movement.

Increases the dancer's ability to hold the leg in high extended poses.

Improves abdominal, thigh, and back strength.

Provides an opportunity to maintain hips level while using the leg in a highly extended position.

Grand Battement Jeté (grahn baht - MAHN zhuh - TAY)

Definition

Large thrown straight beating of the leg. A sequential continuation of battement tendu and battement dégagé. Performed from 1st or 5th positions with a strong upward accent. Can also be performed smoothly at a slow tempo in adagio sequences.

Execution

Perform a battement dégagé, allowing the leg to rise as far as possible without disturbing pelvic alignment.

When doing grand battement derrière, note that the structure of the pelvis only permits a limited leg kick without tilting the torso forward, the result of a strong kicking action. Keep ribs facing directly forward.

Return the leg in a controlled manner to pointe tendue before closing working foot to original position.

Keep height of grand battement within your ability to maintain an extended spine, weight held forward on the supporting leg.

Grand battement at 90° with both thighs well turned out.

Grand battement to 120° is learned after the dancer is strong enough to control pelvic tilt.

Reminders for Good Form

Lift waist, back, and ribs strongly while keeping neck and throat relaxed.

Do not allow arms to wobble, yet avoid stiffness and rigidity.

Brush strongly down and outward before kicking upward.

Both knees remain straight.

Sense a flow of energy from center of back and down across hips.

Lifting the leg from underneath thigh, shoot it upward into space from under the pads of the toes.

Press head upward toward ceiling, especially as leg lowers.

When performing the grand battement derrière, adjust torso forward to balance, like a see-saw, directly through the hip joint.

Purposes

One of the primary components of advanced steps like grand rond de jambe, grand fouetté, and grand jeté.

Develops leg strength and quickness of action.

Limbers the hip joint and leg muscles.

Develops ability to extend the leg to a high level.

Increases hip joint flexibility.

Grand Battement en Clôche (grahn baht - MAHN on klawsh)

Definition

A continuous combination of grand battement front and back, accented like a bell or pendulum. Performed in a series.

Execution

Do a grand battement devant then lower the working leg through 1st position to perform a grand battement derrière.

Continue brushing through 1st position to battement devant.

Reminders for Good Form

Do not drop or tilt the pelvis as the foot brushes through 1st position.

Height of kick should be the same for both devant and derrière.

Maintain strongly vertical torso alignment.

Turn out both legs.

Battement no higher than elasticity of thigh muscles will allow.

Do not permit supporting knee to buckle or ankle of that foot to roll inward in an attempt to kick the leg higher than you have the strength and flexibility to maintain.

Accent the upward motion of the leg.

Purposes

Same as for grand battement.

Develops coordinated leg kicks wth a compensating shift of the center of weight.

---

1. Why do you think so much emphasis is placed on careful execution of these fundamental actions of the leg and foot in barre exercises?
2. What is the purpose of demi and grand plié?
3. Name the French term for a large leg kick.
4. What is the difference between relevé and elevé?

Study Questions

5. The primary circling movement performed by the leg is called _____ . What other positions of the foot and leg are involved as this movement is done?

6. What movements, as described in this chapter, are usually performed slowly and smoothly?

7. What movements described are usually executed in a strongly accented manner?

8. Which exercises emphasize the development of thigh strength?

9. In which exercises does the dancer concentrate upon developing the muscles of the instep, ankle, and toes?

Sample Barre Exercises for Practice

Note: Do each exercise twice, first using the R and again using the L leg. You may either face the barre or stand parallel to it, holding with only one hand.

Meter	*Counts*	*Movements*
1. Plié		
3/4	1–2–3, 2–2–3	demi plié
	3–2–3, 4–2–3	extend knees
	5–2–3, 6–2–3	repeat
	7–2–3, 8–2–3	
	9–2–3, 10–2–3	elevé
	11–2–3, 12–2–3	hold position
	13–2–3, 14–2–3	lower heels
	15–2–3	demi plié
	16–2–3	battement tendu to next position

Note: Perform in 1st, 2nd, and 3rd/5th position.

2. Battement Tendu		
4/4	1–4	battement tendu forward
	2–4	close to 1st position
	3–4	demi plié
	4–4	extend knees
	5–4	repeat tendu forward
	6–4	close to 1st position
	7–4	tendu forward and close
	8–4	repeat tendu and close

Note: Do sequence also to 2nd position and then derrière.

3. Battement Dégagé

2/4	&	battement dégagé to 2nd
	1–2	close to 1st position
	&2–2, &3–2, &4–2	repeat 6 times
	&5–2, &6–2, &7–2	
	&8–2	hold 1st position
	&	battement dégagé devant
	1–2	grand battement en clôche to the back at a low 45° height
2/4	2–3, 3–2, 4–2, 5–2	continue the en clôche,
	6–2, 7–2	alternating devant and derrière
	8–2	close to 1st position

3. Rond de Jambe

3/4	1–2–3, 2–2–3	brush foot devant, circle leg to 2nd position
	3–2–3	hold in pointe tendue 2nd
	4–2–3	continue circle to the back
	5–2–3	hold in pointe tendue derrière
	6–2–3	raise leg slightly off floor
	7–2–3	lower to pointe tendue
	8–2–3	close to 1st position
	1–2–3, 2–2–3	rond de jambe by circling leg front-side-back
	3–2–3, 4–2–3	repeat rond de jambe en dehors
	5–2–3, 6–2–3	repeat
	7–2–3	close to 1st position
	8–2–3	hold reverse all

4. Cambré

3/4	1–2–3, 2–2–3	bend body forward
	3–2–3, 4–2–3	slowly
	5–2–3, 6–2–3	curve torso up to
	7–2–3, 8–2–3	a vertical position

	m 1–16	repeat
	1–2–3, 2–2–3	bring L arm through 2nd to 5th en haut
	3–2–3, 4–2–3	cambré torso to the right
	5–2–3, 6–2–3	return body to vertical and carry arm to 2nd position
	7–2–3	demi plié
	8–2–3	extend knees

5. Retiré and Passé

2/4	1–2	retiré devant
	2–2	hold position
	3–2	lower to 3rd position
	4–2	hold position
	5–2, 6–2, 7–2, 8–2	repeat
	1–2	retiré devant and lower
	2–2, 3–2, 4–2	repeat 3 times
	5–2	retiré
	6–2	continue to passé
	7–2	hold
	8–2	close with foot in back

Note: Face the barre until ability to shift weight is perfected.

6. Grand Battement Lent and Développé

adagio	1–4, 2–4	grand battement
4/4		slowly forward
	3–4	lower to pointe tendue devant
	4–4	hold
	5–4	close to 3rd position
	6–4, 7–2	développé devant
	3–4	hold
	8–4	close to 3rd position
	m 1–8, m 1–8	repeat 2nd position and derrière
	1–4	passé foot from back to front
	2–2	demi plié

	3–4	relevé to 5th position
	3–4, 4–4, 5–4, 6–4	balance in the relevé
	7–4, 8–4	extend legs

7. Grand Battement

4/4	1–4	grand battement to 2nd
	2–4	hold 3rd/5th position
	3–4, 4–4, 5–4, 6–4	repeat grand battement and hold, 2 times
	7–4	battement tendu to 2nd
	8–4	close 3rd/5th derrière
	1–4, 2–4, 3–4, 4–4	repeat to the back
	5–4, 6–4,	
	7–4	battement tendu to 2nd
	8–4	close to 3rd/5th devant

8. Relevé

2/4	1–2	relevé in 1st position
	2–2	hold
	3–2	spring down to a demi plié
	4–2	hold
	5–2, 6–2, 7–2, 8–2	repeat once
	1	relevé
	2	demi plié
	2–2, &3–2, &4–2, &5–2	repeat 4 times
	6–2, 7–2	hold the relevé
	&	demi plié
	8–2	sauté to the next foot position

Note: Face the barre. Execute in 1st, 2nd, and 3rd/5th positions.

Practicing arabesque alongeé fondu. Texas Christian University. (Linda Kaye, photographer)

Elementary Barre Technique

5

After having gained control over the body in the basic movements which constitute barre work, the new dancer is ready to attempt more difficult techniques. The challenge now is to increase muscular strength, coordination, balance, and control of the correctly aligned body which these movements require to insure safe and effortless execution. This is not to say that, prior to attempting these techniques, the dancer must have perfected those barre movements described in Chapter Four. But, the dancer must have experienced and practiced those movements before attempting these new exercises.

Since the movements described here are a direct outgrowth and continuation of those described previously, the analyses will provide that information pertaining directly to the new steps or a variation on the original movement. Think of the steps described in Chapter Four as being the roots. These are the primary branches of an immense tree with its vast network of smaller branches, twigs, and leaves consisting of more and more interesting steps. All ballet steps are related directly to the fundamental movements you are learning now as a beginner.

Further Positions of the Foot

The foot is placed on the ankle in either of two positions: Sur le cou de pied (literally on the neck of the ankle) in which the foot gently wraps around the ankle and coupé in which the foot is held extended.

When the dancer does a plié with the working foot in coupé position, the foot should remain perfectly in line with the calf. This is also called coupé fondu. Turn to Further Battement Variations for an explanation of the fondu action.

Sur le cou de pied devant.

Coupé position devant, arm in en bas.

Coupé position in demi plié or fondu. The pelvis and shoulders should remain squared as the body lowers in plié.

Demi and Grand Plié in Fourth Position

Execution

Begin with both knees extended in semi-open 4th position in which the heels of the feet are opposite 3rd. When your ability to maintain turn out improves, 4th position will be opposite 5th.

Sense rotation in the thighs increasing until the thighs open and the knees bend. Continue deepening the plié keeping the heels pressed on the floor—demi plié position.

For grand plié, continue deepening the bend, allowing heels to lift. At its deepest point, the thighs are parallel to the floor. Press the heels into the floor in order to begin the return to demi plié. Then complete the extension back to the original position.

Reminders for Good Form

Extreme caution must be exercised throughout a plié in 4th position. The knees are vulnerable to strain unless the dancer is strong enough to support the weight of the body.

Do not allow ankles to roll or arches to drop at any time. These errors greatly increase twisting in the knees.

Maintain a strong lift in the pelvis, waist, and middle back.

Be aware of the body lowering and rising directly between both feet.

Purposes

To strengthen turn out and supporting muscles of the pelvis.

To challenge dancer's alignment: the ability to maintain a lifted torso as it lowers and rises while the thighs are held in an extremely turned out position.

Elevé and Relevé Variations

Do you remember the difference between elevé and relevé? When performing the elevé, the dancer rises to the balls of the feet smoothly without the supporting foot changing its location. The body shifts up and over the insteps. During a relevé, on the other hand, the dancer performs a slight spring, drawing the supporting foot quickly under the center of gravity. Emphasize a vertical thrust of the body. In both instances, arrive at full 3/4 height quickly. A strong push downward helps the body get up and over the instep of the supporting foot.

1. In 4th Position. Remembering that this position requires a strong sense of turn out, the dancer concentrates on holding the ankles carefully and centers the weight over the instep. Failure to maintain strongly turned out thighs will result in loss of the rotation altogether. The pelvis, which must remain directly over both feet, will begin to twist.
2. From Two Feet to One Foot.
   Shift weight strongly and directly up and over the supporting leg.

Reminders for Good Form

Press the head directly upward without any change in torso alignment.

Hold lower abdominals and back strongly.

Keep supporting leg from wavering by pulling up strongly on the inner side of the thigh.

Counteract tendency of the pelvis to tilt forward by sensing a strong downward anchoring of the tail bone to the floor.

Keep eye focus in line with the level of the body while feeling an upward pull behind the ears.

Maintain turn out with both thighs opening away from each other.

Execution

Coupé Relevé Devant. Begin in 3rd or 5th position and do a demi plié preparation, Push off both feet until the front foot assumes the coupé position and supporting foot is on high demi pointe. Dancer must shift weight slightly toward the supporting side in order to be perfectly centered over the instep of that foot. Lower to demi plié in 5th position. Can also be performed derrière by doing the coupé with the back foot. Alternate coupé devant and derrière.

Retiré Relevé Devant. Begin as with coupé. Continue drawing the front foot up the front of the calf to a point under the knee cap. Retrace the foot down the calf until toes just about touch the floor. Then relax the foot into 5th position. Can be performed derrière also. It is important to arrive immediately at full elevé extension with the supporting leg. Hold the chest well over the hips as body rises to demi pointe. Keep the pelvis even.

Passé. Begin as with coupé, continuing through retiré. Open the working thigh slightly until the toe is touching the inside of the knee of the supporting leg. This movement is complete when the foot passes to the back of the supporting leg, lowering through retiré derrière and coupé derrière before closing in 5th position. Can be reversed. As the thigh opens to achieve the ultimate height of the passé, shift supporting weight upward and inward toward the center line of gravity. Avoid sinking downward into the supporting hip or dropping the rib cage.

In a retiré relevé, the working foot makes a direct contact with the calf of the supporting leg.

In passé relevé, the working foot moves to the inside of the working leg.

Battement Fondu à Terre   (baht - MAHN FAWN - dew ah TEHR)

Definition

A battement performed with a melting quality.

Execution

Stand in 5th position, R foot devant. Begin with a preparatory movement of battement tendu to 2nd position, close the R foot to sur le cou de pied or coupé devant while L leg simultaneously does a demi plié.

The R leg unfolds forward to end in pointe tendue devant. Fondu with R foot drawing it back into sur le cou de pied and stretch it to pointe tendue 2nd position. Repeat action to the back also.

Battement fondus are performed en l'air at various heights depending upon the dancer's ability to control the pelvis and coordinate the actions of both legs.

Reminders for Good Form

Both legs work together harmoniously.

Emphasize a strongly arched foot throughout.

Do not lift the working knee unless doing the fondu en l'air.

Open both thighs evenly.

Purposes

Develops controlled coordination of the legs.

Increases strength on supporting side of the body and the back.

Emphasizes a smooth movement quality and effortless control of the body.

Battement glissé fondu devant.

Battement glissé fondu à la seconde.

Battement glissé fondu derrière with arm in arabesque position. Notice the focus upward over the line of the arm and wrist.

Battement Frappé (baht - MAHN frap - PAY)

Definition

A striking leg beat.

Execution

Begin with R foot in sur le cou de pied position: Thrust the foot
strongly outward striking the bottom of the toes and the metatarsals
on the floor as the foot brushes outward to dégagé devant.

Quickly return foot to sur le cou de pied.

Repeat to 2nd and derrière.

Note: The R foot does not strike or brush the floor as it returns from
the dégagé. Accent instead the outward action. Can also be performed
to pointe tendue in which the outward strike of the R foot is also
eliminated. The foot then moves directly from sur le cou de pied to the
pointe tendue position.

Reminders for Good Form

Maintain lift on supporting side of body.

Articulate the feet clearly.

Perform the movement with a bright sense of energy.

Do not snap the working knee straight.

Purposes

Trains legs for jumps.

Develops a quickly coordinated response in the working leg and foot.

Increases foot articulation as well as strength.

In frappé, the metatarsals
and toes strike the floor as
the knee extends with a
strong accent.

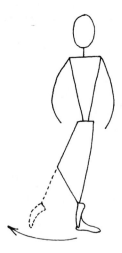

Petit Battement   (PEH - tee baht - MAHN)

Definition
> Small leg beats performed in sur le cou de pied position.

Execution
> Stand with R foot in sur le cou de pied with tips of toes resting on the floor. Open foot slightly so that R heel can pass the heel of the L without touching it.
> Close foot immediately to sur le cou de pied derrière.
> Reverse action to end sur le cou de pied devant.
> Movements are performed rapidly in a continuous series and are usually accented either to the front or the back of the ankle.

Reminders for Good Form
> Remain lifted in the supporting hip.
> Do not elevate or twist hip on the working side.
> Keep back part of working hip and thigh pressed forward.
> Allow heel of working foot to rebound from one ankle position to the next.
> Keep upper chest and back well supported.

Purpose
> Develops brilliant footwork.
> Prepares legs for performing beaten jumps.
> Develops rapidly accented leg and foot movements.

Petit battement is a beat connecting sur le cou de pied devant and derrière.

Assemblé Soutenu (AH - sahm - blay SOOT - new)

Definition
>Drawing the legs together in a sustained manner.

Execution
>Beginning in 5th position, do a battement tendu with the working leg and a demi plié with the supporting leg.

>Extend the supporting leg and simultaneously draw the working leg back to 5th position.

>Repeat to 2nd position and derrière.

>Can also be done with an elevé or relevé as the working leg returns to 5th position as well as with a half or whole pivot, called *assemblé soutenu en tournant.*

Reminders for Good Form
>Do not allow the body to follow the working foot. This pulls your weight off the supporting foot.

>Maintain a strong sense of verticality in the back.

>Sense a flat, wide upper back throughout the movement.

>Feel a strong lift in the inner thigh.

>Stretch toes fully.

>Keep pelvis level throughout.

>Concentrate on opening the supporting thigh on the demi plié.

Purpose
>Develops coordination of the legs.

>Increases the ability of the body to remain centered while in motion.

>Strengthens the inner thigh when drawing legs together.

>Changes the level of the body in space.

In the assemblé soutenu, the preparatory dégagé fondu must be done without tilting the pelvis or shoulders.

Ballonné (BA - lon - nay)

Definition

Literally swollen, but refers to the bouncing, ball-like quality named for a famous male dancer of the late 17th century, Jean Balon. Is part of the allegro repertoire of steps a dancer performs.

Execution

Beginning in 5th position: Dégagé front foot to 2nd and retract it quickly to retiré devant.

Then, lower working foot to 5th position devant.

Ballonné is also done forward and back.

In center allegro combinations, ballonné is performed with a hop.

Note: In ballonné composé, the dancer travels forward, sideward, or backward during the hop. Since the backward action is fairly tricky, you probably will not attempt it during the first year of study.

Reminders for Good Form

Action of the leg occurs with little movement in the pelvis.

Accent the movement of the leg from the dégagé to the retiré position.

Sense slight resistance when bringing foot into retiré.

Draw knife-sharp lines and angles with toes.

Support the waist and back strongly.

Do not drop knee of supporting leg. Lengthen the leg from back of knee up under buttocks.

Purpose

Develops dancer's ability to coordinate an isolated action of the leg from a stable pelvis.

Increases articulated leg actions.

Strengthens muscles controlling turn out.

Increases hip joint flexibility.

 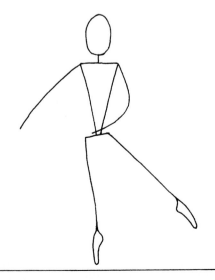

Each ballonné sauté begins and ends in coupé position on a strong demi plié.

At the highpoint of a ballonné sauté, both legs are fully extended. Arms are held quietly for balance.

Rond de Jambe en l'Air   (ROHN de zham on lehr)

Definition

An elliptical circling of the leg at a given extended level in 2nd position.

Execution

From 5th position, dégagé the front foot to 2nd position.

Inscribe an oval with the toes of the working foot slightly touching the calf of the supporting leg and finishing with a return to fully extended leg in 2nd.

En dehors direction is achieved by releasing the foot slightly backward (opening it) as foot moves inward to touch the supporting leg.

En dedans direction is achieved by pressing ankle forward slightly (closing it) as foot moves inward.

Reminders for Good Form

Maintain a stable pelvis.

Sense a strong feeling of lift underneath the working thigh.

Connect the tail bone to the heel of the supporting foot with an imaginary wire.

Press inside ankle bone of working foot forward during the circling action.

Perform this movement with a sense of controlled urgency.

Contract abdominals by sensing a pull of the navel upward under the rib cage.

Purpose

Increases strength in legs and lower back.

Develops stamina for center adagio work.

Works leg extensions.

Strengthens turn out muscles of the hip.

In a rond de jambe en l'air, the thigh is stable and the circling action occurs in the lower leg.

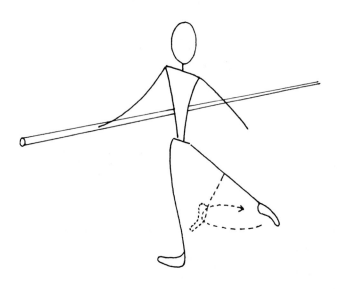

Grand Rond de Jambe   (grahn ROHN duh jahm)

Definition

A full circling of the leg at a fixed extended height off the floor.

Execution

For a grand rond de jambe en dehors, begin in 5th position: Dégagé front foot devant at a given height; circle the leg to 2nd position; and continue to dégagé derrière or arabesque.

Close working leg to 5th position derrière.

Reverse the actions to perform grand rond de jambe en dedans.

Note: Although this technique is usually performed at 90°, the beginner should not exceed 45° until good control of legs, pelvis, and upper torso is achieved.

Reminders for Good Form

Keep working thigh at same height during the entire movement.

Emphasize increasing turn out of the thigh as the impetus for the circling action to begin.

On the grand rond de jambe en dehors, lift thigh very slightly when passing from 2nd position to the back to get over the hip joint smoothly. Do not, however, consciously lift the pelvis.

Do not allow the torso to lean into the barre; maintain a strong sense of verticality in the torso.

Maintain strongly turned out supporting leg.

Avoid allowing the supporting ankle and arch to roll.

Sense that the working knee is attempting to chase the foot as it circles.

Purpose

Develops strength in legs, hips, and back.

Teaches one of the primary rotary actions of the body.

Increases dancer's ability to use the working leg in opposition to the supporting side of the body.

Increases flexibility of ligaments surrounding the hip joint.

Develops a control of the thigh in the hip joint.

Develops hip supporting muscles on the supporting side.

In grand rond de jambe, the torso moves forward over the supporting hip to counterbalance movement of leg from 2nd position to arabesque.

Primary Stretches

So far, only actions requiring a strong vertical spine have been described and analyzed. This is not to say that the ballet dancer rarely bends or twists the torso. Learning how to bend the torso in the three major directions—forward, backward, sideward—is a vital part of every dancer's training. Since the goal is to bend the spine without losing one's vertical orientation to space or without disrupting good body alignment, these movements have been grouped together in one section. The purpose for all stretches is to release tension, increase muscular and joint flexibility, develop suppleness of movement, and enhance a sense of controlled lyricism.

Cambré   (KAM - bray)

Definition
   Arching, curving.

Execution
   Arch the body in a forward or sideward direction on straight legs without any compensating release of the pelvis. The movement will be rather small.
   Usually performed in 1st, 4th, and 5th positions of the feet.
   For more difficult variations, perform also in pointe tendue position, sous-sus, and coupé elevé.

Reminders for Good Form
   Maintain continuity of head and ribs to the hips.
   Press shoulders downward, sensing a widening of the upper back and chest areas.
   Center pelvis over supporting feet.
   Lift abdominals strongly up to the rib cage.
   Relax shoulders, neck, and throat allowing head to react naturally to the bending action.
   Coordinate the bending movement with designated arm movements.

Port de Corps   (por duh kawr)

Definition
   Carriage of the torso. Commonly known as *grand port de bras*.

Execution
   First part—forward bend. Begin by sensing the torso lifting up and out of the hip joints and then bend forward keeping the spine extended.
   When you can no longer maintain the spine fully extended, allow the spine to curve forward until you are standing in an inverted 5th position.
   Retrace movements by first lifting the upper spine and head until the spine is once more fully upright.
   The dancer can also return to an erect standing posture by rolling up or uncurling the spine.

In the forward port de corps, tilt torso at the hip joints. Keep back flat and shoulders even.

Notice the evenness of both shoulders, the width of the back, and the relaxation of the neck.

Full forward port de corps. Legs remain vertical so that the line of gravity passes through major joints of the lower body.

Second part—backbend. Lift the head and chest and arm to 5th
position en haut and arch backward keeping hips facing forward
and centered over the feet.

The backbend is a much smaller movement than the forward bend.

Retain continuity of the head, chest, and arms.

Open arm to 2nd position and retrace actions to an erect posture.

*Port de corps to the back.
The legs are a strong
vertical anchor so that the
back can bend without
being compressed.*

*In all stretches, such as the
demi lunge derrière, reach
away from the center of the
body, extending the lines of
the body.*

Reminders for Good Form

Never release lumbar area of spine or pelvis allowing center of weight
to press backwards onto the heels.

Keep rib cage facing forward.

Maintain head in line with the spine.

Press shoulders downward and outward.

Release extra tension in jaw, neck, and upper shoulder areas.

Maintain actively contracted abdominals muscles.

Few representations of dance training sessions, such as popular films or TV commercials, forget to reveal a dancer stretching the leg on the barre. One might even presume that it was for this very activity that the barre was invented! In truth, barre stretching can be a safe and effective aid to stretching muscles, ligaments, and joints only after the dancer has developed enough strength and flexibility to maintain an aligned body when the ankle has been hooked over it. To attempt stretching on the barre without being able to maintain alignment or without first warming up openly invites strained muscles. Stretching the leg backward in the arabesque line is not recommended for beginners.

Barre Stretches

Port de bras stretch on the barre facing forward.

Side cambré stretch on the barre. The pelvis remains centered as the arm reaches in 5th position en haut.

The harmony of a dancer's line extends from hand through the extended leg in arabesque penché. Ballet West-Christiansen Academy.

Stand diagonally toward the barre with the outside leg approximating grand battement devant on the barre: Bend forward slowly. Continue to reach the body forward, stretching the spine with the working arm in 5th en haut. Open working arm to 2nd as you return to an upright position. Repeat with a sideward bend toward the barre. Alternate forward and sideward bending. 4 times.

Standing in the same position, but with the arm in 2nd: Do a slow demi plié on the supporting leg. Then slowly straighten it. 4 times. Repeat facing the barre, the ankle resting on the barre with the leg in 2nd position.

Again, stand facing the barre in the same position as above: Bring the opposite arm upward from 2nd position to 5th en haut and bend sideward slowly toward the raised leg. Return to a straight position and change hands on the barre. Reach up to 5th and cambré away from the working leg. Can be repeated with supporting leg in demi plié.

Suggested Stretching Exercises

Study Questions

1. What are some of the dangers of performing grand pliés in 4th position?
2. What are the differences between performing an elevé (rise) and a relevé (spring) in 1st position?
3. Describe the correct performing quality for a battement fondu.
4. Which barre movements specifically increase leg strength?
5. Why is a strongly centered alignment of the pelvis so important in ballet?
6. Name the two movements described in this chapter in which the working leg performs a circling action. Draw the shape of the circles which the working foot will make when you do each movement.
7. What makes rond de jambe en l'air different from grand rond de jambe?

A Gift of Wings *by Rosalind Pierson. The Ohio State University. (Ted Rice, photographer)*

Au Milieu
Basic Practice in the Center

6

Exercises at the barre give the dancer the physical foundation to move to the center of the studio where some of the same movements will be repeated, now with new emphasis. Using the head, arms, and some of the many nuances that the human body creates when changing slightly its facing direction gives ballet its fundamental qualities.

Ballet as a performing art designed for viewing in an imaginary theater is learned totally within that special magical framework. Now that the dancer is in the center, every aspect of the body—from head to toe—must be considered in view of an hypothetical audience seated just beyond the mirrors. The directions the body will face, along with head positions, and arm movements (port de bras) during a particular phrase will be carefully defined by your instructor. However, learning to dance means more than sheer rote memorization of foot positions and steps. Dance combines these learned patterns but also must reveal the beauty of the modeled body in space, harmonizing movement perfectly with the dancer's expressive spirit and the rhythms of music.

The reader is asked to refer to Chapter Three for an illustrated description of the basic head and arm positions as well as the primary body facing directions. For the sake of simplicity and clarity, the steps in Chapters Six and Seven have been analyzed facing straight forward. None of the characteristic subtle changes in body facing, head focus, or arm gestures, without which the steps would remain arid and lifeless, has been included. They will be learned during your lessons.

Categories of Center Work

The term used to describe the repetition of certain exercises of the barre in the center. The dancer re-establishes placement and control without the aid of the barre. Thus, the dancer is re-oriented to the freedom of open space on all sides. Demi plié, battement tendu, battement jeté, elevé, and rond de jambe are some of the steps frequently included.

Building a strong sense of centering the body is the emphasis of stationary posture. The dancer may change feet or move slightly in a slow, controlled

Exercises au Milieu
(eg - zer - SIS
oh MIH - lyou)

manner, but the primary concern is development of balance and control. These movements are the keystones to the building of fluidity, "the lack of control which," described the eminent early 20th century ballerina Tamara Karsavina, "makes dancing appear strained, ungraceful and unrhythmical."[1]

Adagio

It is the natural state of man to fall; we do this literally with every step taken. In the adagio section of the lesson the dancer attempts to stop nature, to arrest the tendency to fall off the supporting leg. The dancer's definition of freedom is to attain supreme control over the body so that, as Leonard Bernstein wrote, "A free, heaven-bound leap, proclaiming the divine nature of free man can be taken."[2] In adagio work the body is employed splendidly as a total unit of motion. It strives to unfold in a lyrical manner, breathing life into *andante* passages of music. The dancer expands and retracts slowly into space to overcome gravity, to attain a consummate control of balance, and to create linear designs.

Adagio movements practiced at the barre, such as grand battement lent, rond je jambe en l'air, développé, and grand rond de jambe, and poses like arabesque and attitude are combined with expressive arm movements and simple transitional movements called *pas* (pah). No one will doubt that adages are strenuous and uncompromising in the total effort required of mind and body. But . . . the graceful and poised control which results is well worth the work.

Tours

Turns have a special place all their own. In the early 19th century, dance purists looked down their noses at *pirouettes* (basically a spin on one foot), calling them circus acrobatics. However, audiences, then as now, found the quick snap of a turn exciting to watch; it soon became an integral part of the dancer's compulsory training. At first the student practices and perfects the components of a turn in isolation from other movements. Once a level of competence and composure is attained, various turns are combined with adagio and allegro combinations.

Allegro
(ah - LEG - roh)

Meaning brisk and lively, allegro is divided into two categories. *Demi allegro* focuses on increasing one's agility, clean footwork, and the ability to combine various individually learned movements into phrases of different lengths. *Grand allegro* focuses more specifically on the stamina and strength needed to perform a variety of large jumping movements. In these steps the dancer is propelled upward into space. Agrippina Vaganova has bisected the special nature of allegro into two essential components: *elevation* and *ballon*. "Elevation in the proper sense of the word is a flight," a feat of strength and dexterity.[3]

Ballon is a bounding gazelle-like quality in which the dancer seems to stop time, remaining mysteriously poised in air. Ballon is the result of a careful combination of timing, weight distribution, thrust, breathing, and use of the arms. It results from diligent practice of the allegro techniques as well as from a natural elasticity and ease in jumping. Men particularly work to achieve ballon in their jumps.

The dance lesson can be concluded in a variety of ways depending upon the time allowed or the instructor's goals. Réverènce, dating back to the knight's chivalrous manner of greeting a fellow gentleman, recalls our traditional cavalier roots. It also serves as a reminder that the class is a triune gift involving teacher, student, and accompanist. The dancer learns a graciously poised manner for accepting the applause of an appreciative audience, thanking them for having attended the performance. Refer to the end of this chapter for a description.

Cultivate a pleasant, elegant expression when performing réverènce, savoring this small yet not unimportant moment at the conclusion of your class. Additionally, take this well-deserved opportunity to cool down and bring the body to an easy state before returning to your daily affairs.

Combinations of previously learned movements joined into a flowing pattern constitute the very heart of each lesson. When ready for this unique challenge, the dancer attains the fulfilling sensation of what dancing is all about. Try to gain an organic flow of all movements as they are being learned. Part of the challenge that learning various steps imposes is to allow those steps to have individual values. Never color your movement palette all white. Instead, approach each of the following pas as a new color, the combination of which will become the spectrum of your experience in dance.

Many of the initial sequences you will learn are traditional; they define ballet as a specific style of motional expression. They help you learn appropriate natural rhythmic phrasing and timing of specific balletic movements. Certain head and arm movements with these steps will be performed consistently, whenever those steps are danced. One example is the use of the head. Generally it is focused toward the direction in which you will move, as in pas balancé, chassé, and glissade. When balance is required, the head will turn and incline slightly toward the supporting leg, as in coupé, pas de bourré, and jeté sauté.

Although the repertoire of dance steps is rather narrow, when compared to the actual range of movement possibilities available to the human body, performing these patterns to different meters, melodies, tempi, and directions will instill a wide vocabulary of stylized movement. This vocabulary is the requisite technical training for every dancer, from the novice to the premier danseur. Much as the music student practices standard classical chord progressions and études as training to play any kind of composition, so does the classically trained dancer experience these steps as part of the daily class.

The two most frequently used poses in ballet are *arabesque* and *attitude*. Performed in a variety of positions (refer to Chapter 3), these poses are "still points" in time and space. They are also performed in motion, as when doing a sauté or relevé. In the case of the advanced dancer, they can be combined with a spin on one leg called an arabesque pirouette.

1st arabesque.

Arabesque (AHR - a - besk)

Definition

An Arabian curved line design popularized by 18th century French artists.

Execution

Stand on a fully extended R leg and extend L to the back in a line elevated sequentially from pointe tendue through dégagé.

Depending upon the height of the extended L leg, the torso tilts forward evenly with back well arched, abdomen lifted, and waist held firmly.

The pelvis adjusts as the L leg approaches 90° or above, but the back and rib cage remain centered.

Press the body weight well forward over the instep of the supporting R foot.

The body should create a long, harmonious curve from fingertips of the forward arm through focus of the eyes and backward to the tips of the extended toes. Sandra Hammond refers to arabesque as "the true test of a dancer's line."[4]

Note: Illustrated are the four standard arabesque lines of the Vaganova-Russian school, as well as the familiar third arabesque of the Cecchetti-Italian school.

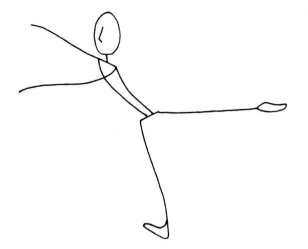

2nd arabesque.

3rd arabesque.

Cecchetti 3rd arabesque.

4th arabesque.

Reminders for Good Form

Focus carefully upward and outward over the wrist of the forward arm.

Practice the arabesque initially à terre, with the back foot in pointe tendue derrière.

Do not twist shoulders back toward raised leg. Sense, instead, a squareness to the direction you are facing.

Maintain well turned out working leg without leaning over the supporting hip.

Maintain a strongly lifted supporting leg.

Lengthen the waist line, elevating rib cage.

Attitude Derrière   (at - tih - TEWD)

Definition

A pose supposedly developed by Carlo Blasis in the 1820s, after a statue of Mercury executed by Giovanni da Bologna. The dancer balances on one leg with the other leg extended behind with the knee bent from 45° - 90°.

Execution

Stand on a strongly lifted supporting L leg with the R leg bent at an angle.

Extreme emphasis is placed on turn out of the R thigh so that the knee is at least on the same plane as the foot. R arm is curved en haut and the L arm is extended to 2nd position. It is usually executed in a croisé or éffacé facing direction. The R leg is lifted behind the body, but attitude devant can be performed also.

For beginners, lift the leg only 45° until an understanding of the position and balance required is gained.

*Attitude derrière . . .
notice the horizontal
alignment of the thigh.*

*Attitude croisé derrière
with the arms in Cecchetti
3rd arabesque position.*

Reminders for Good Form

Sense a strong spiraling action through the back, R hip, and R foot.

Allow body to balance evenly on L leg, lifting back of L knee and thigh strongly into hip socket area. Beware of pushing weight back into the L knee.

Do not tilt torso and pelvis sideward over L hip.

Support pose with strong abdominals and a taut waist.

Lift upward strongly under R thigh to help support that leg.

Press shoulders downward, but do not twist or pinch them.

Transitional Movements

Connecting the various poses, jumps, and turns is a series of pas or locomotor steps carrying the dancer from one place to another. Like other techniques, these steps are learned and practiced by themselves in a series before being joined with other steps to form combinations or phrases. Interestingly, these steps have evolved from the 17th century court dances of Louis XIV and demonstrate the aristocratic lineage of classical ballet.

Pas Marché (pa mar - SHAY)

Definition

Walking in a regal manner.

Execution

With feet turned out, weight is shifted sequentially from toe to ball with each step.

Barely allow the heel to come in contact with the floor.

Stretch foot forward, with toes about 2″ above the floor before taking step.

Chassé (sha - SAY)

Definition

A sliding step in which one foot chases the other.

Execution

Begin in 5th position, R foot forward (vis. 1): Extend R foot sideward (vis. 2) to 2nd position, demi plié (vis. 3).

Spring slightly pulling the L foot into 5th position in the air (vis. 4).

Land in demi plié on the L, R foot in coupé.

Arms are held either in 2nd position or in 3rd en avant.

Note: This step can be performed on an éffacé or croisé diagonal, moving forward (en avant) or backward (en arrière), as well as sideward (de côté).

Chassé de côté to the right.

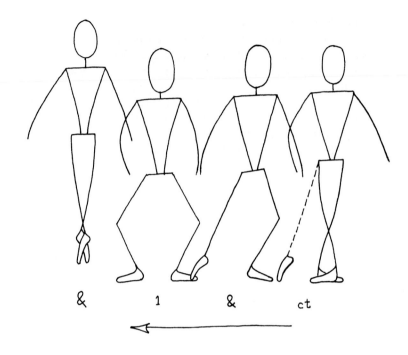

Reminders for Good Form

    Keep pelvis even throughout the chassé.

    Avoid a see-saw or a noticeable galloping action of the body.

    Be sure to use the feet to push legs off floor.

    Draw feet quickly to 5th position in the air.

    Maintain relaxed arms, but do not allow them to wobble.

Temps Lié (tahn lee - AY)

Definition

    Literally, smoothly connected time or a thick feeling like honey.

    Changing weight from one foot to another in a slow, controlled manner through 2nd or 4th positions.

Execution

    Begin with R foot in 5th position, facing forward: Battement tendu R foot to 2nd position.

    Lower body to demi plié in 2nd, then rise onto a straight R leg with L in pointe tendue seconde.

    Close to 5th position, L foot forward. Repeat to L side.

    Note: Temps lié is performed both croisé and éffacé devant and derrière. As proficiency and smooth articulation of each position is gained, vary the step by replacing the battement tendu and pointe tendue with dégagé and développé.

Reminders for Good Form

    Sense strong upward lift under buttocks at all times.

    Open both legs evenly in the transitional demi plié.

    The body is truly balanced first on one foot, then on two, and finally on one foot again before closing to 5th position.

    Harmonize use of the arms and legs to achieve a smooth performance quality.

    Keep hips up and well forward over supporting foot.

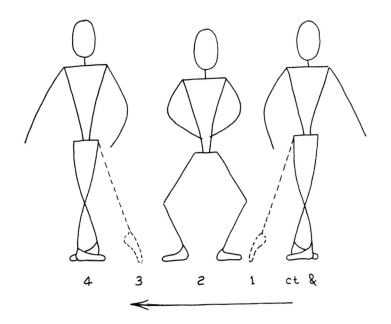

In temps lié de côté, shift weight through demi plié in 2nd position. When traveling forward or backward, shift weight through 4th position.

Pas Tombé (pah tom - BAY)

Definition

    Any action in which the weight falls from one foot to another in contrast to stepping or leaping from one foot to another.

Execution

    Begin in 5th position, R foot devant demi pointe: Slide R foot to 2nd position with a simultaneous lowering to demi plié on the R foot, keeping the L leg extended.

    Close to 5th position, both legs extended, R foot forward.

        Note: Can be performed in all directions and from positions with the working foot lifted off the floor, such as piqué, passé, arabesque, and attitude.

In pas tombé, "fall" into a
small lunge éffacé devant.

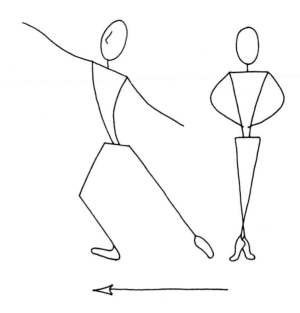

Reminders for Good Form
> Maintain pelvis centered over insteps of feet.
> Do not drop weight or allow knees and arches to roll inward as body
> lowers to plié, a fondu action.
> Rib cage or waist remains lifted.
> Tilt head subtly into the direction of the tombé to aid the smoothness
> of falling action.

Pas de Bourré Dessous   (pah duh bu - RAY de - S00)

Definition
> A dance step of three steps in which the first step is performed
> underneath 5th position.

Execution
> Begin in 5th position, L foot devant: (&) Dégagé R foot to 2nd
> position on a demi plié.
> (1) Close foot to 5th position derrière on demi pointe.
> (2) Remaining on demi pointe, L foot opens to 1st position.
> (3) Close R foot to 5th devant and demi plié.
> For pas de bourré dessus (pah duh bu - RAY de - SYEW), simply
> reverse the action. Dégagé the front foot to the side during a demi
> plié, then close it to 5th devant opening the back foot to 1st position
> on demi pointe. Finish by closing the R foot to 5th position derrière
> in demi plié.

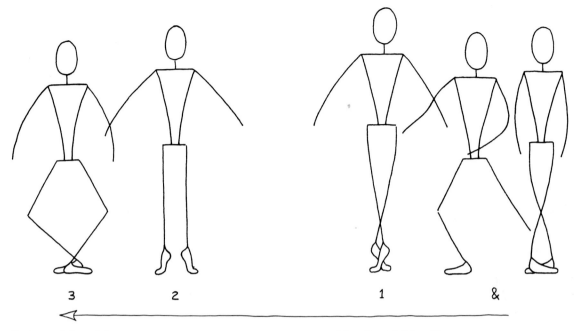

3	2	1	&

Begin pas de bourré dessous
with a dégagé fondu.

Move through 1st position
demi pointe with extended
knees before closing into
5th position, demi plié.

Reminders for Good Form
> Maintain weight over supporting foot.
> Do not allow pelvis to relax or knees and ankles to roll inward during
> plié.
> Lift waistline strongly.
> Lift under thighs and fully point feet to support the working leg.
> Focus with a slightly tilted head toward working leg side to begin step.

Variations
> Do an outside turn with pas de bourré dessous.
> Pick up working foot to coupé or retiré height for a staccato feeling.

Glissade (GLI - sahd)

Definition
> A sliding action performed with an uneven rhythmic flow.

Execution
> Begin in 5th position, L foot devant: Demi plié and focus diagonally to
> R.
> Slide R foot to 2nd position and spring lightly so that toes are slightly
> off floor in 2nd position.

Land on R foot in fondu, L leg fully extended.

Close quickly to 5th, L foot devant. Travel in a R sideways direction.

Reminders for Good Form

Isolate the legs and feet from the pelvis to prevent see-saw action.

Control spring and descent for smoothness.

Spring lightly.

Extend both legs fully.

Do not allow weight to drop or knees and arches to roll inward.

Press heels into floor during the demi plié for maximum stretch of the Achilles tendon and calf muscles.

Variation

Leading from the front foot through 2nd position and traveling forward or backward, leading with the front or back foot respectively.

Glissade uses a slight spring to shift weight through 2nd position with a smooth, flowing transition.

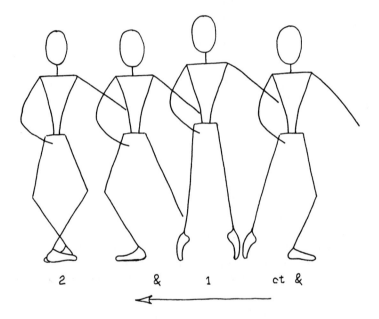

2   &   1   ct &

Posé to Piqué Position   (PO - zay pee - KAY)

Definition

A posé on a straight supporting leg in which the working leg holds a high retiré derrière. Performed with an abrupt puncturing quality.

Execution

Begin with R foot in 5th position devant: R leg does a small dégagé éffacé devant on demi plié.

Step forward onto R foot, L leg draws quickly to high retiré derrière. Position of waking foot depends upon placement and strength.

R arm remains in 3rd position en avant.

Close L foot to 5th position derrière.

Note: Once proficiency is attained, posé directly up to demi pointe on supporting foot. Posé into such poses as arabesque and attitude. A more difficult variation is to reverse the direction, traveling backward (en arrière). (See also section on turns, Chapter 7.)

Sense a strong vertical line through the supporting leg during posé piqué.

Reminders for Good Form

Emphasize turn out of both legs, without allowing hips to twist.

Do not relax downward or backward on the demi plié.

Spring slightly to transfer weight from the demi plié onto a straight supporting leg.

Maintain pelvis forward over insteps.

Coupé Dessous   (koo - PAY de - SOO)

Definition

A cutting under action which changes the feet.

Execution

Begin with L foot pointe tendue derrière: Slice L foot into 5th position.

Complete movement by doing a fondu on L foot extending R foot éffacé devant.

Reverse action for coupé dessus (koo - PAY de SYEW).

Variations

Close to 5th position demi pointe, releasing working foot to dégagé at
45° angle.

Perform a demi développé as leg extends in the fondu.

Spring from coupé devant to coupé derrière for a coupé sauté.

Note: Coupé is frequently done before a step or a chassé as a
preparation step or as part of a *contretemps*.

During coupé dessous, the
dancer cuts one foot out
from the other.

Reminders for Good Form:

Attempt to keep pelvis stationary and weight centered over feet.

Replace feet exactly through 5th position. The legs are cutting out
each other.

Support underneath the thighs to help prevent tendency of legs to pull
hip as they extend alternately.

Do not allow waist to sag down into the plié.

Pas Balancé   (pah bah - lahn - SAY)

Definition

A rocking step consisting of three steps performed to ¾ music and
derived from the waltz.

Execution

Balancé de côté—From 5th position R foot in front: (&) Fondu on L
slightly as R extends to 2nd position.

(1) Fall (tombé) onto R foot, close L into coupé position derrière.

(2) Immediately step up onto L demi pointe allowing the tip of the R
    foot to draw into 5th position.
(3) Transfer weight to the R foot, releasing the L foot to coupé
    derrière. Alternate sides.

Notes: Can also be performed en avant, en arrière, as well as turning
(*en tourant*), doing one-half turn on each balancé.

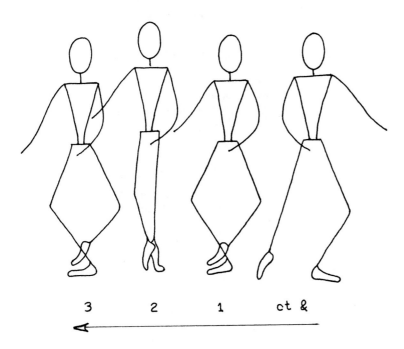

A balancé is a kind of waltz step. Notice that the arm changes with the step.

3   2   1   ct &

Reminders for Good Form
    Keep legs well turned out.
    Be sure to shift weight on each step or count.
    Perform fondus softly.
    Allow arm movements to arrive into position a little late, enhancing the
        melting, romantic feeling.

Sous-sus (siew - SIEW)

Definition
    Literally under-over.

Execution
    A pose in tight 5th position on high demi pointe. Begin in 5th position:
        Step forward to demi pointe and close both feet into a tight 5th
        position.
    Arms usually draw up to 5th en haut from 2nd through 1st en avant.

Sous-sus croisé, arms in
5th position en haut.

Reminders for Good Form

    Press inner part of thighs together to assist in balance.

    Sense strong rotation of both legs from behind the pelvis and deep in
       the hip joint.

    Balance upper torso up and over insteps of feet, knees fully extended.

    Do not allow ankles to wobble.

Primary Demi Allegro Movements

Springing into the air landing on the original foot (a hop or temps levé), landing on both feet (a jump or sauté), or landing on the other foot (a leap or jeté) are joyously exuberant experiences. Allegro is a term borrowed from music meaning brisk or lively. It embodies a quickness of spirit, a movement quality which takes practice. Development of strength in the legs, feet, and back, rhythmic sense of timing, and control of breathing are needed.

    The key to all sauté, jeté, or temps levé actions is the strong upward push under the insteps and pelvis during the beginning and concluding plié. The dancer gains a powerful thrust to spring into the air while maintaining control over the force of gravity on the descent. Keep heels pressing into the floor throughout the beginning and concluding demi plié. Thrust the legs straight to propel the body into the air without snapping the back or knees. Think of a hard hand ball rebounding strongly and buoyantly off the floor as you practice allegro sequences. The pelvis should never drop back on the heels, and the spine should work to remain vertical, especially during plié.

Avoid the tendency to lurch backward with the upper chest as you are propelled into the air. Focus toward the side of the landing foot to help center the weight over that foot. And keep arm gestures simple, smoothly controlling them with shoulders held downward. Support your arms from the center of the back, preventing wobbling which will disrupt the center of balance.

Again, as with the barre exercises, those allegro steps which are most appropriate to the earliest lessons in ballet are being described. These, with the exception of the last one, are sautés; they begin and end on both feet. Both jeté and temps levé will be easier to learn and perfect after you have developed strength and control over your body.

Sauté (soh - TAY)

Definition

A jump from two feet, landing on both feet.

Execution

Spring vertically, maintaining the legs in a position relative to the beginning foot position.

Thrust strongly away from the floor using a deep demi plié and fully extended legs and feet in the air.

Do in 1st, 2nd, and 5th positions. (See Chapter 8 for variations.)

Sauté in 2nd position.

Reminders for Good Form

Hold abdominals and waist strongly.

Do arm gestures simply without tension or stiffness.

Allow focus to rise slightly as body springs into the air.

Inhale as body rises into the air for added lightness.

Lift up on back of knees and extend toes fully in the air.

Avoid tendency to throw chest backward in the air or to release hips backward in demi plié.

Soubresaut   (soo - bruh - SOH)

Definition

A sudden jump in 5th position.

Execution

Begin in 5th position: Spring vertically into the air pulling feet into sous-sus.

End in 5th position, demi plié.

Move slightly forward (en avant), backward (en arrière), or sideward (de côté).

Extend legs and feet fully during soubresaut.

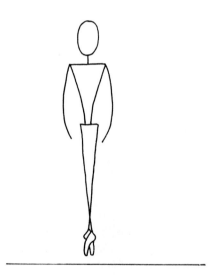

Reminders for Good Form

Keep weight centered over both feet.

Emphasize turn out.

In the air, the legs should look like one unit.

Do not release hips on demi plié or shove chin forward in order to move en avant. The body travels because of the direction of the thrust initiated by the feet.

Support arches and ankles during demi plié.

Changement des Pieds (shahnzh - MAHN duh pee - AY)

Definition

A jump changing the feet through 5th position.

Execution

Begin in 5th position demi plié, R foot front.

Spring vertically into the air allowing feet to approximate 1st position.

Close R foot back in demi plié.

Note: In *petit changement,* spring only high enough to allow tips of toes to graze the floor. For *grand changement,* thrust body as high as possible into the air, allowing thighs to open to 2nd position in the air, also known as *ciseaux* (seez - OH)

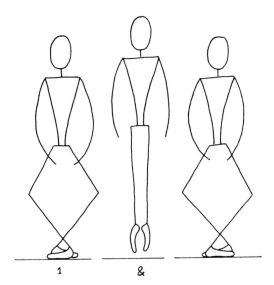

Do not let the pelvis twist or ankles roll in changement.

1   &

Reminders for Good Form

Do not overcross the 5th position on the landing.

Turn out both legs equally in the air to prevent the pelvis from twisting.

Press into floor evenly with both feet on the demi plié.

Sissonne Simple (see - SOHN SEHM - pluh)

Definition

Thought to be named for the inventor of the step, Comte de Sissonne, sissonne is a leap from two feet landing on one foot. It can be performed with a variety of ending positions, such as coupé, dégagé, arabesque, or attitude.

Execution

Begin as with soubresaut: Instead of ending on two feet, land either on the front foot with the back foot in coupé position (sissonne simple derrière), or land on the back foot with the front foot in coupé position (sissonne simple devant).

In sissonne simple, the opposition of the arm to the leg will help the dancer maintain balance.

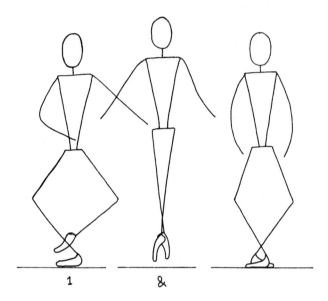

1   &

Tours

Turns or *tours* (toors) require learning a special technique called "spotting" which has a number of very interesting functions. Besides assisting the inner ear to help decrease dizziness, this trick of strongly focusing the eyes throughout a turn, on a specific point at eye level, helps the dancer develop momentum to achieve multiple spins on one foot. The dancer instinctively concentrates on the verticality of the head and spine. In addition, spotting achieves a brilliant finished visual look for each turn.

The first turns you will experience will be on both feet and are best thought of as pivots instead of spins. In these, as well as the turns described in Chapter Seven, one must lift thighs, abdominals, and waistline strongly. Turn with as little force from the arms as possible.

Think of the turn in three sections: (1) preparation, (2) turning position, and (3) recovery. Care and thought must be taken on each phase of a turn to insure that you are performing all the positions and movements correctly. The first concern should be the problem of balance. Momentum is something built into the turn itself, so flinging the arms or twisting ribs and hips are unnecessary, causing a barrier to success. The preparation positions for outside and inside turns will be practiced by themselves before adding the actual turn.

Preparation for an outside pirouette. Some teachers prefer the back leg to be straight.

Preparation position for an inside pirouette.

Soutenu en Dedans en Tournant
(SOOT - new ahn TOOR - nahn)

Definition
>A complete pivot on two feet in the direction of the forward foot.

Execution
>Begin in 5th position, R foot forward: Fondu on R foot and brush L to 2nd position, arms in 2nd.
>
>Slice L foot to a tight 5th position, simultaneously rising to demi pointe and pivoting completely to finish facing forward, R foot devant.
>
>Arms close to either 1st en avant or 5th en haut.
>
>End in a strong demi plié.
>
>*Note:* This is often introduced as a half turn.

Pas de Bourré en Tournant en Dehors

Definition

A pas de bourré dessous with a complete outside turn.

Execution

Perform a pas de bourré dessous with a half turn on each of the first two steps and a demi plié in 5th position as the third step.

The pivot steps are done in the direction of the back foot.

In other words, if the first step of the pas de bourré is done on the L foot, the entire turn sequence turns to the L.

Reverse all for pas de bourré en tournant en dedans.

Révèrence

As described at the beginning of this chapter, the révèrence is a courtly bow or curtsey, a fitting close to your lesson. A great variety of bows exist. Described is a simple form for women and men.

Execution:

Women

Begin in 5th position, R foot devant: Temps lié to the R, opening the arms to 2nd position. Cross the L foot behind but keep the weight on the R foot. Curtsey deeply, dipping the head and arms without losing sight of the audience. Recover to a vertical posture and focus straight ahead. Repeat to other side.

Men

Begin with R foot in 5th position: Temps lié to the R using a shallow demi plié. Close L foot to 3rd position opening arms to 2nd. Lower R arm while dropping head and shoulders forward slightly. Recover to a vertical posture focusing straight forward.

Study Questions

1. How do movements practiced at the barre help you dance in the center?
2. What are the meanings as used in dance of the following musical terms: adagio and allegro?
3. A courtly bow which usually ends a ballet class is called _____ .
4. Define the following jumps: sauté, jeté, temps levé.
5. The two posed shapes in which the working leg is raised behind the body are called _____ and _____ .
6. Visualize mentally the various transitional steps the dancer can perform in order to move through space: chassé, pas marché, temps lié, pas tombé, and glissade.
7. How are a chassé and a glissade different from each other?
8. What step in ballet is most similar to the waltz?
9. Why should the dancer maintain a strong back with knees aligned over the insteps during jumping movements?

10. What role does plié play in performing good jumps?
11. In a changement, what changes?
12. What is spotting? How is it used during turns?
13. If someone in your class was having difficulty with balancing in a piqué posé, what kinds of reminders would you give that friend?

End Notes

1. Tamara Karsavina, *Classical Ballet: The Flow of Movement,* (New York: Macmillan Co., 1962), p. 15.
2. Leonard Bernstein, *The Infinite Variety of Music,* (New York: Simon & Schuster, 1966), p. 115.
3. Agrippina Vaganova, *Basic Principles of Classical Ballet,* (New York: Dover Publications, 1969), p. 69.
4. Sandra Hammond, *Ballet Basics,* (Palo Alto: National Press Books, 1976), p. 76.

Grand jeté en avant. Texas
Christian University. (Linda
Kaye, photographer)

Elementary Steps au Milieu

7

You should begin to understand now the progressive development of ballet technique and style. From practicing simple to complex arrangements of steps, your body and mind have acquired the necessary strength and coordination to assemble them into elementary steps. Comprising center *enchainements,* these steps impart a sense of dancing, helping you feel the continuity of purpose to the exercises you have practiced. You will be able to recognize these movements when watching ballet performances, too. What should be understood is that the word "elementary" does not necessarily mean simple. Rather, steps like *pas de basque* or *chainé tour* are the very backbone of every dancer's technique.

It is assumed that you have been training for a while before attempting these movements. The reminders for good form—1) holding the head high; 2) extending the arms from the center of the back; 3) elevating the back and chest cavity; 4) emphasizing turn out through a spiraling action beginning from behind the thigh; 5) articulating the feet fully; and 6) maintaining positions with the least amount of effort by aligning the body efficiently around the center line of gravity—must certainly be continued when doing the following steps. The reminders provided for each will consist only of those new or special problems relative to the successful execution of that movement.

This chapter is divided into traditional allegro steps of elevation, further transitional or connecting movements, and turns on one and two feet. For simpler forms of these steps, consult the previous chapter. Concluding this chapter is a series of study questions to assist in your review of what you have learned.

Allegro Steps

Remember that all elevation steps are categorized and named for the basic skill involved: jumping—sauté, hopping—temps levé, leaping—jeté, and leaping from two feet to one foot—sissonne. The following allegro steps have been analyzed under their "family" names so that this unique relationship is more obvious. This process will make it easier to learn the movement itself and its underlying technical principle, while establishing a foundation from which to learn more advanced steps.

Sauté (sew - TAY) Literally means tossed. Emphasis is upon vertical height with a springing quality.

Échappé (ay - shah - PAY)

Definition

To escape; both feet thrusting away from 5th position simultaneously to 2nd or 4th position.

Execution

Begin in 5th position, R foot devant: Jump into the air, holding the legs in 5th position (sous-sus).

As the body descends, open feet to 2nd position and end in demi plié.

Reverse the process: Spring into the air, holding 2nd position and land in 5th position, demi plié, L foot devant.

Note: Each échappé consists of both sections of the technique and is also performed as an échappé relevé in which the dancer springs lightly with the tips of toes sliding on the floor to 2nd position, demi pointe. The toes release as feet slide back into 5th position, demi pointe. It is performed to 4th position as a sauté and relevé.

The first action of the échappé is a spring from 5th position with thighs held together tightly.

Reminders for Good Form
> Move both legs equally, evenly, and simultaneously.
> Hold ankles strongly.
> Do not allow ankles or knees to roll inward on demi plié.
> Maintain base of spine pulled downward throughout to prevent a buck-action in the torso.

Coupé (koo - PAY)

Definition
> Cutting action performed with a jump.

Execution
> Perform a succession of coupé over (dessus) and under (dessous) with a jump into sous-sus in the air between each one.
> Can be thought of as a succession of sissonne simple performed without closing to 5th position between each one.
> See section on turns for a description of coupé entournant.

Reminders for Good Form
> Keep shoulders and rib cage held easily.
> Think of springing up over 5th position and landing on the same spot.
> Rebound evenly off of each foot, concentrating on opening the working thigh strongly.
> Jump strongly to sous-sus position in the air on each coupé sauté.
> Hold arms, shoulders, and head firmly yet not stiffly.

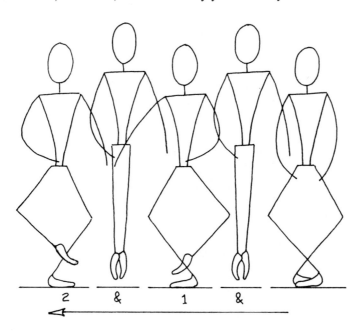

Coupé sauté, dessous and dessus.

Assemblé Dessus   (ah - sahm - BLAY duh - SYOU)

Definition

An assembling of the legs in the air, usually preceded by a dégagé action of the working leg.

Execution

Begin in 5th position, R foot devant: Brush L foot to 2nd position on a demi plié.

Spring into the air as L leg reaches demi height.

Assemblé the L leg back to 5th position in the air (sous-sus) before landing in 5th position, L foot devant.

Reverse actions for assemblé dessus.

Variations

Assemblé porté in which the dancer allows momentum to carry him forward (en avant), sideward (de côté), or backward (en arrière).

Assemblé devant and assemblé derrière in which the working leg performs the dégagé action forward or backward respectively, and the dancer remains in the same place.

Grand assemblé in which the working leg brushes up to a height of 90°.

Reminders for Good Form

Practice the timing of both legs extending fully on the spring and closing before landing.

Brush floor fully with foot, extending toes and ankles in the air.

In assemblé derrière, feel a strong undercurve as the working leg pushes into the floor.

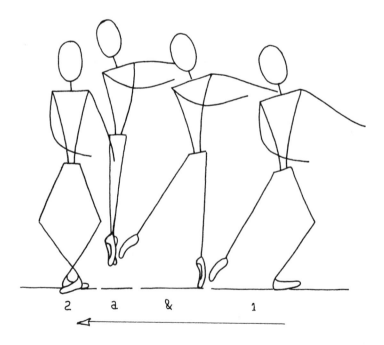

Allow a breath action in the arms to remind you to inhale deeply on
the brush and spring to gain a greater sensation of buoyancy.
Lift torso to avoid pitching forward in the demi plié or backward while
in the air.

Ballonné Simple   (ba - law - NAY SEM - pluh)

Temps Levé Steps

Definition

A ball-like rebounding hop while doing a simultaneous battement
dégagé with the working leg.

Execution

Begin in 5th position, demi plié, R foot devant. Battement dégagé R
foot to 2nd and spring vertically.
Both legs are fully extended at the highest point of the hop.
Land on the L foot in demi plié with the R in coupé position derrière.
Reverse procedure hopping on the L foot with the R foot in coupé
position devant.

Note: Can also be performed as ballonné simple devant (working foot
will dégagé forward), ballonné simple derrière (working foot will
degagé backward), and ballonné composé (ballonné simple devant,
chassé en avant, and close back foot to 5th position).

1   &

Ballonné steps are
performed with an upward
rebounding accent, adding
to their brilliance.

Reminders for Good Form
> Spring off of both feet evenly.
> Accent upward elevation by extending both legs fully at highest point of the hop.
> Do not allow working hip to wobble.
> Hold waist and upper back strongly.
> Contract abdominals without tilting the pelvis.
> Avoid tension in neck and shoulders.

Temps Levé (tahn luh - VAY)

Definition
> Literally time elevated. A hop with the working leg either held in a specific position or allowed to move as in the ballonné sauté. Can be performed alone or in a series.

Execution
> Assume the desired position with weight centered carefully over the instep of the supporting foot.
> Demi plié quickly pressing the whole foot into the floor, allowing weight to shift slightly forward, chest fully over instep of support-foot.
> Spring into the air high enough to fully extend the toes.
> Finish with a controlled demi plié on the same foot.

Variations
> The variety of temps levé steps is vast; one usually begins with the foot held in coupé position.
> Variations, named for the position of the working leg, include dégagé, ballonné, arabesque, rond de jambe, rond de jambe en l'air, and attitude.

Temps levé in arabesque position, also known as arabesque sauté.

Reminders for Good Form

Sense a strong, steel rod running from hip to tips of the toes when airborn.

Do not allow thighs, knees, and ankles of either leg to collapse on recovery.

Focus on some point slightly higher than eye level.

Maintain the arms smoothly in the given position without "clutching" at the space around you.

Inhale deeply on the push-off without pitching the rib cage forward.

Jeté (zhuh - TAY)

Jeté Steps

Definition

A throwing action, a leap: the body is tossed into the air from one foot to the other. The working leg actively assists the leap with some kind of battement or kicking action.

Execution

Two of the most common forms of jeté are described below. The key element in all jeté is the changing of the feet.

Jeté sauté dessus: Begin in 5th position demi plié, R foot devant.

L foot does a strong dégagé action to 2nd position.

As the L foot almost reaches full extension, spring into the air landing on the L foot, demi plié, with the R foot in coupé position derrière. Repeat with the R foot.

For jeté sauté dessous, reverse the description.

In jeté sauté devant, execute the dégagé devant, and for jeté sauté derrière, dégagé the working foot backward.

Jeté dessus is a vertical leaping step.

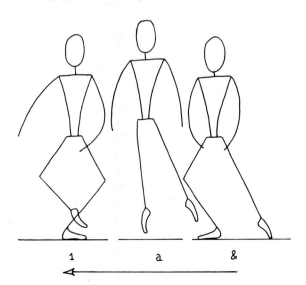

1   a   &

Grand jeté en avant: One of the most spectacular steps in ballet.

Exhilarating to perform, the dancer experiences a momentary state of weightlessness.

Usually performed after some kind of lead-up preparation step, such as a chassé or pas couru (three running steps), the dancer does a grand battement devant which propels the body into the air.

Immediately do a grand battement derrière with the back leg so that you approximate a split in the air.

Land on the leading leg, holding the back leg in an arabesque.

Permit the back and pelvis to tip forward enough to balance, like a teeter board, over the instep of the supporting foot in a solid demi plié.

Reminders for Good Form

Lift the center of the waist.

Extend both legs and feet fully in the air.

Inhale on the ascent to help gain a sense of buoyancy.

Contract abdominals strongly.

Isolate the strong kicking action of the thigh from the pelvis and torso to prevent a rocking horse action.

A strong battement is one of the keys to a successful grand jeté.

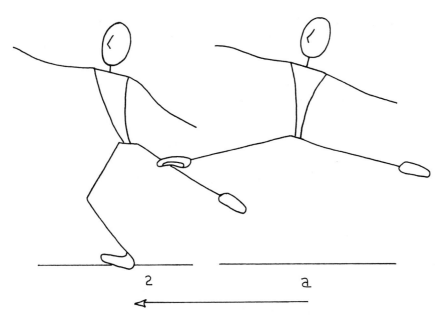

Allow torso to tilt forward over the supporting thigh when landing, holding back strongly.

2   a

Coordinate head focus with arm actions along with the lift-off and
    descent to gain maximum elevation with minimum effort.
Keep rib cage strongly lifted, particularly on the landing.
Do not allow knees and pelvis to sink into the floor.

Sissonne (see - SAWN)

Sissonne Steps

Definition

As a category of allegro by itself, sissonne begins on two feet and ends
    on one. If the working leg remains extended, it is called sissonne
    ouverte or open. If the emphasis is placed on closing the working leg to
    5th position almost simultaneously with the leap, it is called sissonne
    fermé, closed.

Execution

Review the execution for sissonne simple from the previous chapter.
The working foot, in this more advanced version, performs a battement
    to a specific direction.
Described here is the basic version in which the working leg extends to
    demi height in a sideward direction.
Sissonne can be done to retiré, arabesque, and attitude with the leg
    extending to the front, side, or back. Ouverte (oo - VEHRT) and
    fermé (fehr - MAY) are the two varieties of sissonne.

Sissonne ouverte de côté. Begin with R foot devant in 5th position. Spring directly into the air traveling slightly to the R as the L leg extends to 2nd position. Land on R in demi plié, holding L in dégagé seconde. Close L through pointe tendue to 5th position, ending with L foot devant. Repeat to the L side.

In sissonne ouverte, extend the working leg fully before closing to 5th position.

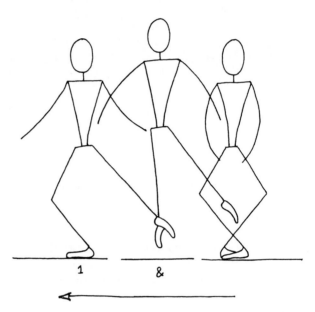

Sissonne fermé de côté. Perform as above, but close working foot immediately to 5th.

In sissonne fermé de côté, spring directly into dégagé.

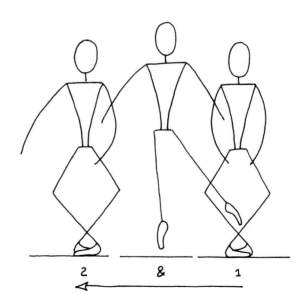

Sissonne fermé or ouverte en avant. Perform as above but in a forward direction.

Sissonne fermé or ouverte en arrière. Perform as above but in a backward direction.

Reminders for Good Form

Sense the body working as a single unit.

Push off the floor strongly with both feet.

Allow eye focus to establish the direction of the sissonne.

Remember to incline head slightly toward the supporting side.

Arms must remain in line with the torso; do not allow them to lose their shape or flop around.

Much of your time in the center will consist of learning some of the connecting movements which give class combinations style and character. Highly rhythmical in nature, mostly descendants of folk or court dancing steps, these movements are fun to do and fan fresh air into the work of building a strong technical foundation. The body moves in playful harmony with the rhythms of the music to challenge time and space. Sometimes dancers refer to these steps as "breathers" simply because one can relax; the body reacts easily and naturally to the energy and pulse of the music.

Notice how each of these little steps is actually a development or an expansion of the basic step patterns. Therefore, only the execution and reminders for good form are included.

Transitional Steps

Demi Contretemps   (deh - MEE kahn - truh - TAHN)

Execution

Begin with R foot front in 5th position: Do a sissonne simple derrière which ends with weight on the R foot in demi plié and the L foot in coupé position derrière.

Slide L foot through 1st position into a chassé croisé en avant.

End with weight on L with R foot in pointe tendue croisé derrière.

Close R to 5th position. Repeat to the other side.

Note the important head and arm patterns which will help turn the torso to face an angle at the end of the step.

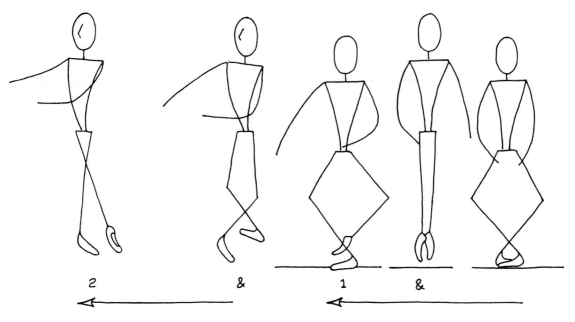

2

&

1

&

Finish with a slide through
4th position to pointe
tendue derrière.

In demi contretemps, spring
lightly into sous-sus in the
air.

Reminders for Good Form
> Articulate feet carefully.
> Do not roll knee and ankle of sliding foot inward during the chassé.
> Coordinate the arms with the movements of the legs.
> Do not overcross foot positions on the chassé; keep sliding foot directly
> in line with 1st position.

Failli   (fai - YEE)

Execution
> Begin in 5th position, R front, facing croisé: Demi plié, soubresaut
> turning torso to éffacé devant, L shoulder coming forward.
> Open L leg to demi arabesque landing on R in demi plié.
> L foot immediately does a chassé croisé en avant.
> Torso and head incline slightly over L shoulder to the audience.
> The step ends with the dancer standing on L with R foot in pointe
> tendue croise derrière.
> Notice the similarity to demi contretemps.

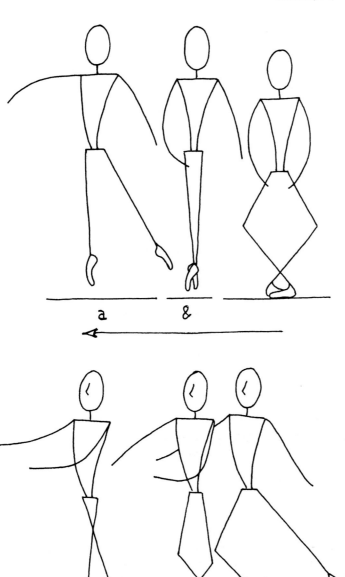

Compare the differences between failli and demi contretemps.

Failli is usually performed in combination with a chassé.

Reminders for Good Form

> Spring into air quickly and lengthen out the musical time (*ritard*) on the chassé croisé.
>
> Retain the extension of the back leg during the chassé action.
>
> Coordinate arms with legs for a smooth flow of movement.
>
> Spring up on soubresaut (count &) only high enough to stretch the feet before descending into the chassé.
>
> The accent of this step is one the chassé action (count 1) and the final pointe tendue croisé pose (count 2).

Sissonne Tombé   (see - SOHN tom - BAY)

Execution

> From demi plié, R foot devant, do a sissonne simple devant.
>
> As dancer lands on L with R in coupé position devant, fall forward diagonally to éffacé on the R in a lunge.
>
> Usually followed by a L pas de bourré.
>
> *Note:* Can also be done with the falling action taken to croisé devant, de côté, or croisé and éffacé derrière directions.

Reminders for Good Form

> Do not anticipate the tombé, thereby failing to articulate feet on the sissonne simple.
>
> Lean into the tombé so that transfer of weight from the L to the R foot is complete.
>
> Maintain the pelvis in a fully centered, held position. Avoid the tendency to tilt the pelvis during the tombé part of the step.

Pas Marché   (pah mar - SHAY)

Execution

> Walk regally high on demi pointe with feet passing through 1st position.

Variation

> Pas couru (pah koo - RHEW), a running preparation for a leap in which two steps are done on demi pointe and the third is done in demi plié.
>
> While the rhythm for a pas marché is even, a pas couru is performed with counts 1 & 2 or & a 1.

Reminders for Good Form

> Reach feet forward well turned out with knees almost straight.
>
> Do not bob up and down; retain a smooth elegant posture.
>
> Articulate the feet carefully without appearing to mince or prance.

Pas de Basque en Avant   (pah duh BASK on ah - VAHN)

Execution

From 5th position, R foot devant: (1) Rond de jambe en dehors the R
to 2nd position and step to the side.
(2) Close L to 1st position immediately sliding it croisé en avant.
(3) Finish by stepping on L with R foot in pointe tendue croisé
derrière. Alternate sides.
Reverse it by traveling backwards for pas de basque en arrière.

3   2

Épaulement, the subtle
movements of the head and
shoulders, gives pas de
basque its special look.

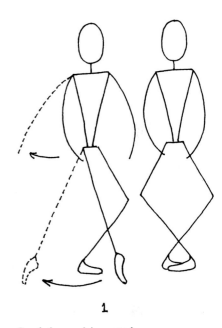

1

Pas de basque joins a rond
de jambe action with a step.

Reminders for Good Form

Sense a floating lift of weight off of feet on count 1.
Do not roll ankles during the chassé forward.
Stress turn out of the supporting leg.
Execute the linear design of this step clearly.
Coordinate arms with action of the legs for a clear, smooth
performance.

Pas de Chat   (pah duh SHAH)

Definition

A bright, brilliant step of the cat.

Execution

Begin in 5th position, R foot devant: Demi plié, then spring into the air with a quick retiré derrière of the L foot.

Immediately retiré the R leg so that at the high point of the spring, both legs are in passé, toes almost touching.

Recover onto L foot in demi plié, holding R foot in retiré.

Immediately close R to 5th position.

Reminders for Good Form

Practice a strong, knife-like quality with the legs.

Emphasize turn out and foot articulation throughout.

Lean slightly toward line of direction.

Move directly sideward.

Avoid tendency to lose turn out of the closing leg.

Tours

Nothing is more exciting for both the dancer and the audience than to see dancers spinning effortlessly around their center lines of gravity. Turns, done first on both and then on one foot, must be practiced patiently and diligently; they are not something we are accustomed to doing in everyday life. It is in the turn, however, that a number of hurdles appear as each one of us discovers how our body wants to "behave" during it. Subsequently, one learns and perfects different strategies—like the height of the arm position or force of the push off—to enhance the ability to turn.

Be sure to review the concept of spotting, the technique of focusing on a single point and turning or flipping the head quickly during the turn. Spotting must become second nature to the dancer; its importance to the success of turns goes without saying.

Piqué en Dedans   (pee - KAY on duh DAHN)

Execution

Turning inward toward the center of gravity, the dancer steps out onto the R on a high demi pointe, L held in piqué derrière or devant.

Immediately spin in the same direction as the supporting leg.

After completing one turn, coupé onto the L and dégagé R diagonally toward the direction of the turn.

Usually performed in a series.

Repeat to the other direction.

Hold the working foot tightly in the supporting leg in a piqué turn.

Reminders for Good Form

Step directly up onto R foot without buckling R knee or ankle.

Keep body absolutely vertical during the spin on the R foot.

Bring L leg up to retiré position quickly.

Pull arms directly into 1st position as the weight is shifted onto the R foot.

Avoid tendency to whip in order to gain momentum for the turn. Instead, press forward the back and hip of the side opposite to the direction of the turn.

Chainé (sha - NAY)

Definition

Literally means chain.

Execution

This step is performed in a series usually on a diagonal line.

Step out onto R demi pointe, arms in 2nd.

Immediately close L into 1st position on demi pointe, then close arms to 1st en avant, making a half turn.

Use this momentum to continue stepping alternately on R and L, making a half turn on each step.

Progress on a straight line path.

Spot vigorously into the direction of the turn, but hold the arms fairly still throughout the series of chainé.

Reminders for Good Form

Sense the whole body working as a single unit.

Remain high on demi pointe with thighs and abdomen lifted, and knees fully extended.

Study Questions

1. The allegro step which means to escape is _____ . Which basic foot positions does the dancer move through during this step?
2. Coupé is a cutting action; describe how this step is performed.
3. Name sequentially the ballet movements you do during barre exercises which are incorporated into ballonné simple.
4. What is the purpose of demi plié during allegro work?
5. Why is grand jeté such a popular step for dancers?
6. A leap which begins on two feet and ends on one foot is called a _____ . Name the three directions in which this step is performed: _____ , _____ , and _____ .
7. How are transitional steps used in classical dance?
8. Compare failli and sissonne tombé. How are these steps similar or different?
9. Why is alignment of the pelvis so important a factor in good allegro dancing?
10. Name the step of the cat. What kind of quality does the dancer adopt when doing this step?
11. What is the most difficult part about doing a piqué turn?

August Bournonville's
Konservatoriet, *1849. Texas*
Woman's University Dance
Repertory Theatre.
(Jennifer Collins,
photographer)

Dance Traditions Before 1900

8

People are remarkable social beings. In every age meaningful life styles have been sculpted from a variety of experiences. The development of dance as a unique, precise theatrical art form has been in process since the beginnings of recorded history. Nourished by an ever more complex set of social institutions, dance in both its theater and ritual form has been an important human statement.

The earliest civilizations, such as the pre-Christian dynasties of China, India, and Egypt, have let us know that dance was accepted in its dichotomous roles: as pagan entertainment and as religious ritual. In its sacred use, dancers codified natural gestural language, intensifying motion with specific mimetic interpretations of Nature; while, as entertainment, the sensual and spectacular were exploited in breathtaking feats of wonder.

Over the centuries, the various guises for dance have gradually converged. Contemporary theatrical dance elements are a culmination of the ancients' worship of their various gods, medieval *commedia dell'arte* pantomimes, court masques of the Renaissance, technical virtuosity of the Romantics' bounding from earth, and investigations of the inner man and perception by early 20th century Realists.

Lincoln Kirstein said it best. "Art is not an imitation of nature. It arose from the breaking down and intensification of religious essences . . . dancing is a constant reminder of life and death."[1] Briefly described are some of the events and concepts which have helped to shape the contemporary ballet scene.

During the voluptuous Medieval Age, life was circumscribed on the one hand by the intellectualism of a scholastic rediscovery of Classical thought models and on the other by the most horrible bestiality of serfdom and of religious wars (the first Crusade began in 1096). Dancing gave the newly converted a way to worship the Lord as well as to find release from the horrors of poverty, starvation, and servitude.

Medieval Panorama

"Dansomania" as a phenomenon surfaced as a kind of desperate panacea. Frenzied dancing lifted people momentarily out of their viciously hopeless existence. A primary example from our own age were the marathon dancers of the 1930s who danced non-stop for days at a time for cash prizes.

If many peasants coped with life by dancing uncontrollably, the emerging fuedal aristocracy was entrenched in rigid social patterns. Characterized by the Courts of Love, the result was an intricate tapestry of feudal court life. Opened up was an idyllic fantasy world of love songs, idealized bliss, and romantic interludes. Refinement through the pursuit of fashionable recreational pastimes was a primary emphasis. Complex rules for posture, behavior, and deportment gave rise to codified dance rituals to match the melodic tones of the *chanson,* a Medieval ballad song form.

Growing out of the troubadors' *chansons* was a new poetry enriched secular music. The clear melody line created a need for movement invention to match the embroidery of the pulses and dynamics of these songs. Ushered in was a new kind of artist, the dancing master.

One of the earliest known teachers was mid-15th century Guglielmo Ebreo, famous for his compositions devised for the Florentine court of Lorenzo the Magnificent. Courtiers had to perform under rigorous standards while they participated in the elaborate entertainments. Whole careers weighed in the balance of a wrongly flicked wrist. Ebreo's precise dances achieved an elegance and a standard which at once became theatrical.

As the Humanist strivings during the Renaissance opened the age to a scientific understanding of the geometrical unity of the Universe, so did increasingly influential dancing masters, like Ebreo, liken the art of dance to a manifestation of the absolute cosmos. "Dancing is an action, showing outwardly the spiritual movements which must agree with those measures and perfect concords of harmony which, through our hearing and with earthly joy, descend into one's intellect."[2]

What a vibrant age it was! Gone was the aesthetic severity to which the doomed Medieval man was bound. The Renaissance exalted in the abundant human potential and the vastness of the earth's natural resources. Pioneers set out to explore them both. It was a society which felt itself to be in complete control over its world.

The intricate floor patterns and movement inflections of the dances required courtiers to attain that same mastery which defined the seemingly flawless intertwining of Nature, Mankind, and the Universe. Court entertainments were modeled upon the myths of classical Greece, "the true and honest virtues." Invested were fortunes to recreate elaborate sea battles in flooded ballrooms, to construct monumental gilt pageant cars for processions, or to devise fabulous costume balls.

Feeding this vast appetite for entertainment was the dancing master. Absorbed in the perfection of Romanesque architecture, the curving intricacies of cavalry formations, and the recently developed use of perspective in painting, he devised a multitude to stately *basse danses,* brisk *saltarellos,* lively *galliards,* and haughty *pavannes.* Courtiers practiced constantly. Formal social dance was not a recreation. The presentation of pageants and fêtes took second place only to warfare and diplomacy as the primary function of the courts.

While the strictures of court-imposed cultural standards suppressed natural expression, a fascinating phenomenon took root. Small troupes consisting of dancers, singers, mimes, jugglers, and tumblers began tramping across Italy; later, they continued across Europe. The aristocracy found these *commedia dell'arte* troupes both amusing and threatening. Although welcomed and banished by turns, these improvisational companies grew in popularity, the last vestiges not dying out until the late 18th century.

Broad, often bawdy, humor was the emphasis of the repertoire which dug deeply into universal problems of bureaucratic red-tape, philandering husbands, greedy doctors, and stupid country bumpkins. Commedia dell' arte characterizations so epitomized the human condition that they are used as theatrical devices even today.

The Preeminence of France

Italian forerunners of opera and practices in theatre and architecture were transplanted to France in the 16th century when Catherine de Medici married the future Henri II. In 1581, her sumptuous court entertainment, lasting hours and costing a king's ransom, "Ballet Comique de la Royne" was the centerpiece of the wedding celebration for the Queen's nephew, the Duc de Joyeuse. Greco-Roman mythology and Old Testament morality were the cornerstones of an aristocratically tasteful plot, retelling the legend of Circe. Every embellishment of this extravaganza was related to the theme; thus, the unification of divertissement, aria, costume, and music became the standard for future court festivities, known as *ballets de cour.* It was a landmark in the development of ballet.

The published libretto found its way into the hands of Inigo Jones, the great English architect and court machinist, and Ben Jonson, the eminent playwright. Their collaborations in early 17th century England created a whole new genre: the *masque.* Jonson's poetic dialogue and Jones' imaginative stage effects and atmospheric lighting fed the Elizabethan fondness for wondrous illusory images.

Monumental collaborations involving choreography, music, song, costumes, and special effects reached their zenith under the reign of Louis XIV (1643–1715) in France. Serving the Sun King, as he was respectfully called, were the talents of composer-producer Jean Baptiste Lully (1632–1687), comedic playwright Moliere (1622–1673), scenic designer Jean-Louis Berain (1638–1711), and dancer-ballet master Pierre Beauchamps (1636–1711). A true professional opera-ballet resulted.

In 1661, the King requested Beauchamps to establish *l'Academie royale de danse* in order to systematize body positions and *pas,* or steps, as well as to create a foundation for professional instruction. In the letters of patent for the *Academie,* Louis stated that dance was "one of the most valuable and useful arts for nobles and others who have the honor to enter our presence. . . ."[3]

Shortly thereafter *l'Academie royale de musique* (1669) was inaugurated; these two institutions were united in 1672 under the title *l'Academie royale de musique et de danse.* A more academic, organized structure resulted in the taking over of dancing roles in the court entertainments by a growing corps of professionals.

Early Dance Writers

The year 1700 brought with it two important innovations.

First was the delicate opera-ballet form developed by Jean Philippe Rameau (1683–1764). In his productions, dancers were required to sing and dance expertly. Pantomimic gestures augmented the arias and recitatives while the lengthy dance divertissements marked a happy climax to the light entertainment.

Second was the publication of Raoul Auger Feuillet's *Choréographie* in 1701, ushering in a new age of dance writing. Although a manuscript on dance notation was prepared by Pierre Beauchamps almost 25 years earlier, it was Feuillet's writings which popularized this new invention. Notation permitted the dissemination of social dance steps from one country to the next and strengthened French influence on the teaching of dance. A number of steps, like chassé, jeté, and pirouette are still performed just about as Feuillet described. France remained the model for both the etiquette and science of dance until a pale of creative weariness enveloped the Parisian theater world following the Napoleonic Revolution in 1789.

In 1712, John Weaver's *Essay towards a History of Dancing* established dance as a bona fide communicative art form combining the ritual of gesture with the technical demands of theatre. "Stage dancing," Weaver expounded, "was at first design'd for Imitation; to explain Things conceiv'd in the Mind, by the Gestures and Motions of the Body . . . so that the Spectator might perfectly understand the Performer." Right on Weaver's heels came Pierre Rameau's *The Dancing Master* (1725). Rameau codified the now traditional five feet and arm positions and defined the primary training methodology. Even today, Rameau's rules form the foundation of the ballet class.

First Stars

The growing corps of professional dancers led naturally to the emergence of stellar performers. One of the earliest male celebrities was Jean Ballon (1676–1739), known for his light footwork and the soaring rebounding quality of his "capers." Dancing along with him was Mlle. Françoise Prevost (1680?–1741) who, after making her debut in Lully's opera *Atys* in 1699, went on to become the first full-fledged ballerina.

Once the ladies were permitted access to the stage, they quickly rose to stardom capturing the imagination of the era, the wealthy bourgeoisie audiences.

One of these was Marie Sallé (1707–1756). Never a brilliant technician, her performance of the Statue in *Pygmalion* (1734) will live for all time as a turning point in the art of dance. Expressive movement clothed in a natural drapery costume befitting a Greek goddess brought forth a new model for theatrical dance costuming: to dress each character according to time and place instead of convention.

The acclaimed virtuosity of another danseuse, Marie de Cupis Camargo (1710–1770), gained a large following. Because of her vigor and lightness, she was known particularly for her elevation and brilliant entrechats. Exploiting her technical assets, Camargo shortened her gowns to mid-calf and adopted a softer, low-heeled shoe.

Jean Dauberval (1742–1806) was an acclaimed demi-character dancer although best known to us as the choreographer of the second oldest ballet still performed, *La Fille mal Gardée* (1789). Another notable male dancer was Gaetano Vestris, the first dancer bold enough to remove his mask when

Gaetano Vestris shown performing Noverre's Medea et Jason *in a staging from 1781. (Courtesy of the Dance Collection, the New York Public Library at Lincoln Center, Astor, Lenox and Tilden Foundations.)*

he appeared in Noverre's *Medea et Jason* (1763) in Stuttgart. Truly as conceited as he was a gifted virtuoso, Vestris called himself "le dieu de la danse," yet his talent could not be denied; even Parliament closed its sessions whenever he performed.

The Influence of Noverre

All of these dancers were greatly influenced by the most formidable individual of the pre-Romantic age, a man remembered neither for his dancing nor his choreography: Jean Georges Noverre (1727–1810). Through his writings, primarily *Letters on Dancing and Ballet* (1760), Noverre came to be known as the Great Reformer.

Ballet d'action was the term he coined to describe a balletic composition which was unified by a logical story line, forwarded through natural, expressive gesture, and supported by the music, costumes, and scenery. Noverre argued adamantly against meaningless displays of gymnastic virtuosity. Instead, the dancer should reflect human passions in steps "arranged with intelligence and artistry . . . that they correspond to the action and movement of the dancer's soul."[4]

Nature, in its raw form, was for the early Romantic but a rough cut diamond still in need of the craftsmanship of the jeweler (choreographer) to reveal its ultimate beauty. Noverre wrote that "a fine picture is but the image of nature; a finished ballet is nature herself. . . ."[5] Almost 150 years later a Russian ballet historian concluded that "he aided the choreographer to set a man, his fate, his actions, his trials, into the centre of the ballet."[6]

Dauberval's *La Fille mal Gardeé* (1789) is a primary example of a successful interplay of Noverre's principles. Lise and Colas, the two heartsick lovers, are real people, not idealized Olympian figures. Their youthful efforts to marry in spite of Lise's mother's negotiations to marry off her beautful daughter to the wealthy farmer's imbecilic son, Alain, constitute the comic plot. Here now was a ballet in which the various elements of plot, location, characterization, and use of dance technique were welded into a cohesive entity. In 1828 the ballet was finally introduced to Parisian audiences where it was acclaimed.

Early 19th Century Romanticism

The French Revolution brought an abrupt halt to all older court-related dance forms. The Frenchman's innate passion for the theater could not be stifled, so into the void stepped the sensual fantasy world of such German writers as Goethe, Heine, and Schiller. Now it was the middle class who held the reins of culture. The bourgeoisie was fervent in its interest in folk mythology, sentimentality, and supernatural images. From these literary sources, ballets and vaudeville plays provided a release from the growing pains of unrelentless industrial urbanism.

Noverre's precepts were furthered in Italy by Salvatore Vigano (1767–1821) whose work is best described by one word, *choreodrama.* His dances were founded upon the need to express a dramtic idea through plastique, communicative gesture rather than abstract ballet technique or stereotyped movements and poses.

Later, another Italian, Carlo Blasis (1797–1878) furthered Noverre's definitions of the ways in which the body should be used in classical dance. His models for line and shape were Greek friezes and statuary; his neo-classical outlook resulted in vivacious naturalistic movements à la Grecque.

Blasis' major treatise, *Code of Terpsichore* (1828), addressed artistic issues and provided students and teachers alike with advice. "Nothing is of greater importance in dancing than frequent practice; . . . no other art demands a stricter attention in this particular."[7] He paid special attention to the dancer's placement. "In your performance be correct; in your steps, brilliant and light; in every attitude, natural and elegant."[8]

The Golden Age of Ballet

As heavy brocade costumes gave way to softer Greek stylized chitons, a virtual explosion in the technical range for both men and women resulted in an era known as "The Golden Age." Romanticism, as a philosophical, artistic, and literary concept, revolutionized all of life. Everyone was touched by it, not least of all the ballet. Luminous describes the many dancers who performed during the 19th century.

The first true representative of romanticism in ballet was Phillippe Taglioni's *La Sylphide* (1832), which established firmly the choreographic model when the curtain opened to reveal an ethereal sylph poised gently next to a sleeping Scotsman, James. The mystical creature of the supernatural world, danced by Taglioni's daughter Marie, utterly captivated the imagination of a generation which felt itself captured by urban blight and recovering from the horrors of the French Revolution. Marie was the epitome of the sylvan, lyric, romantic dancer. "She lifted one up from this earth," witnessed the great 19th century Danish choreographer, August Bournonville. "Her divine dancing could make one weep: I saw Terpsichore realized in her person."[9] Théophile Gautier called her dancing sacred. Taglioni's evocative port de bras and her newly developed pointe technique (the first fully documented ballet to use pointe work was Didelot's *Floré et Zephre* in 1795) epitomized the age of women dancers.

Balletomanes clamored for more. Others included Carlotta Grisi (1817–1909) and Augusta Maywood (1825–1876). Fanny Elssler (1810–1884) was known as a pagan dancer for her voluptuous folk dances, and Fanny Cerrito (1817–1909), Taglioni's closest rival, was felt to combine the ethereal style of Taglioni and the spark of Elssler, out-dancing Marie in sheer technique. No one surpassed Marie for her unique "Taglionism," a liquidy smooth quality which remained the illusive ideal for Romantic ballerinas.

Théophile Gautier (1811–1872), critic for *La Presse,* more than any other individual, provided the inspiration from which the whole era found its substance. He encouraged ballet masters to borrow popular literary themes like supernatural manifestations, folk tales, mystic poetry, and the mystery of moonlight. His opinions on dancers and ballets were on the tip of everyone's tongue. For example, he viewed male dancers as rough-hewn, hairy-chested, and awkward, an anathema to the divine dance. Gautier commented quite unabashedly on the sensuality vs. the spirituality of particular *danseuses.* Legendary standards for feminine artistry evolved from his flowery reviews. Gautier served unofficially as both press agent and supreme cultural trend setter for Parisian balletomanes.

Along with Jean Coralli, Gautier co-authored the libretto for *Giselle* in 1841, the quintessence of the Romantic Age. Focused upon the perils of unrequited and jilted love, it was founded upon the Germanic tales of the *wilis* (restless spirits of maidens who died on the eve of their weddings). Gautier placed the setting for his two act ballet in two separate realms. The real world of Act 1 is the setting for the heartbreaking story of Giselle's girlish happiness turning into deception, despair, and death. In counterbalance is Act 2, set in the world of supernatural folk superstitions, a forest glen lit by an eerie moonlit

Contemporary pas de deux in a Romantic style. Brigham Young University Theatre Ballet.

night, and peopled by a corps of angry wilis out to revenge themselves upon the first man who dares to pass through the forest.

Albrecht's guilt-ridden elegy at Giselle's grave is interrupted by these maidens. His fate is to dance to his death, but he is spared by the intervention of the newest addition to the wilis' corps, Giselle. The purity and strength of her love uplifts him during his lengthy solo until the first light of dawn forces these night wandering ladies to scurry for cover. Carlotta Grisi, Gautier's beloved ideal dancers, captivated Paris with her interpretation of Giselle, a role created especially for her. The ballet, surviving in a version mounted in St. Petersburg by Marius Petipa in 1885, remains to this day one of the yardsticks by which flowering ballerinas are judged.

As eyes strained to see the various new female stars of the ballet, the number of roles and consequently the number of male dancers dropped steadily. Gautier led the attack: "Nothing is more abominable than a man who displays a red neck, great muscular arms . . . his whole frame shaken with leaps and pirouettes."[10] Reviled publicly, what *danseurs* remained were the few who could impress the critics.

August Bournonville (1805–1879), himself one of the few respected male dancers, complained that in Paris men were only looked upon as porters for the ladies. Following a brief career with the Paris Opera, Bournonville returned to Copenhagen to take up the reins of the Royal Danish Ballet, a position he retained almost constantly until 1877. It is his version of *La Sylphide* (1836), produced four years after Taglioni's, which is still performed. Bournonville had learned the old French technique. So it is in his ballets that one may glimpse the style of dancing we call Romantic. *Napoli* (1842), *Konservatoriet* (1849), and *A Folk Tale* (1854) are three of his works in which this style of pure dancing is displayed.

Three other luminaries of the period were Jules Perrot (1810–1892), Carlotta Grisi's husband, whom British historian Ivor Guest considers the greatest choreographer of the time. His strongly dramatic stories and his use of dance movement expressed the action of the plot. He was able to gather on one stage four of the greatest ballerinas of the day in a divertissement created at the request of Queen Victoria: "Pas de Quatre" (1845). The dancers included Taglioni, Grisi, Cerrito, and Lucile Grahn, a competitor of Elssler. Then completing her historic tour of the United States, Fanny was not available for the historic performance, so Grahn took her place.

Second in this trio is Lucien Petipa (1815–1898), older brother of Marius who would become the most formidable choreographer of the late 19th century. Lucien was a danseur noble, a dancer whose physique paralleled the perfection of the Greek gods, and was greatly admired for his immaculate style and elegance.

Arthur Saint-Leon (1821–1870) was another good dancer, but he is remembered chiefly today for a single work, *Coppelia or the Girl with the Enamel Eyes* (1870), a ballet he completed shortly before his death. Marking officially the close of the glorious Romantic Era, *Coppelia* is known for its charming dances and masterly Delibes score. By the end of the century, the idea of using folk-inspired stories interspersed with supernatural wonderment had lost its freshness. Parisian audiences cared only for diversion, so Saint-Leon made little attempt to join the dances together in a logical sequence or to bring cohesion to his far-fetched plot. A life-like doll, Coppelia, infatuates Franz who is already engaged to Swanhilda. (Originally, Franz was played *en travestie* as was the accepted practice.) In Act 2, Coppelia seems to come to life. But it is only the impetuous Swanhilda, who has sneaked into Dr. Coppelius' toy shop and dressed in the doll's costume. Dr. Coppelius' disappointment is eased by a sack of gold and everyone lives on happily. Dancing was not an art but a mindless entertainment of a bored, pseudocultured Parisian society.

As far back as the reign of Peter the Great (1672–1725), the French ballet was incorporated into the court life of Russia. St. Petersburg came to be a monument to the prevailing influence of Louis XIV's elaborate style. Peter established a court theater, and during Empress Anne's reign (1693–1740) an academy for dance was founded.

The Ballet in Russia

Catherine the Great (1762–1796) was an extravagant arts supporter. The seeds of the Russian style, to emerge about 75 years later, were sown when a Frenchman, Le Picq, and an Italian, Angiolini, were teamed up to create both a repertoire and a corps of dancers for the Czarina. Most vital to the development of ballet was the tenure of Charles Didelot (1767–1837). Brought to the Russian capital as ballet master of the Imperial Theater in 1801, he remained to choreograph an amazing number of ballets until his death in 1837.

Following Didelot's death, Jules Perrot arrived ten years later and remained as ballet master until 1859, setting most of his famous repertoire on the St. Petersburg company.

It is, however, to Marius Petipa (1819–1910) upon whom most of the honor is heaped in regards to the flowering of the Russian Imperial Ballet. He had arrived in St. Petersburg with Jules Perrot in 1848, but it was not until 1862 that Petipa was finally promoted to First Ballet Master. Having at his elbow the teaching talents of Christian Johannson (1817–1910) and Lev Ivanov (1834–1901), Petipa created his innovative ballets, transcending style and accepted forms, to evolve an architectural line coupled with massive energy. Rightly, he is called the "father of the classic ballet."

A completely new concept of choreography, based upon symmetry of form and line and exploiting the expanded virtuosic gifts permitted by the blocked pointe shoe, evolved from the Czar's mandate to create fitting court entertainments. Sprouting from the roots of detailed French refinement and Italian love for dramatic characterization colored by flamboyant showmanship, Petipa's ballets were monumental in scale and demanding in technique. "Once more," wrote Alexander Bland, "ballet took on the role of conspicuous expensiveness; spectacle was welded to romantic feelings."[11] Petipa's productions cost fortunes and used most of the 100 member company.

Well-known to Western audiences are his collaborations with P. I. Tchaikovsky: *The Nutcracker* (1892) and *The Sleeping Beauty* (1890). A hard taskmaster was Petipa, he gave strict instructions for meter, number of measures, as well as mood. Evidentally Tchaikovsky thrived under such a severe creative environment. Theirs was an inspired relationship which gave the world the most perfect, unified scores composed for the dance up to that time. An earlier ballet, *Swan Lake* (it had failed in its 1877 Moscow premier with a less talented Julius Reisinger), was restaged and reworked musically in 1895.

Pierrina Legnani, dazzling audiences with her tours de force, in costume for Swan Lake. *(Courtesy of the Dance Collection, the New York Public Library at Lincoln Center, Astor, Lenox and Tilden Foundations.)*

An ailing Petipa was assisted by Lev Ivanov, responsible for the poetic beauty of the second and fourth acts.

Petipa's choreographic method eventually stagnated into a formula—dramatic emotional situations colored by the supernatural, charming peasant folk-derived dances, meteoric technical feats for the soloists, eye-catching picture post-card sets and costumes. Two Italian ballerinas are remembered for their roles in his ballets. Pierrina Legnani (1863–1923) triumphed in the dual role of Odette/Odile in *Swan Lake,* as much for her dazzling 32 fouetté pirouettes as for her interpretation of the role. A pupil of the aging Carlo Blasis, Carlotta Brianzi (1867–1930) captured everyone's heart as Aurora in *The Sleeping Beauty.*

Today, Petipa's ballets remain popular much for the same reasons that they succeeded in St. Petersburg. As one contemporary male dancer recently admitted, the classical repertoire is extremely revealing of one's imperfections; "they're frightening to do." Each sequence of movement, so clearly following the sheer academic rules, demands nothing short of the best technique.

The theatre, with the impending revolution in Russia and the conflagration of the First World War, was ripe for change. Impressionist painters had been fragmenting experiential effects of light on their canvases since the 1870s, while Freudian psychology gave birth to a new generation of thinkers and writers. This inward approach to man's ego and sense of reality was reflected in the tragic plays of Chekov and Ibsen. Composers, like Ravel, Debussey, Stravinsky, and Satie, influenced by the driving rhythmic pulses of primitive tribes, would strike out to new unmelodic paths.

Dance could not remain a viable art form unless it too dug deeply into its core of motional potentialities to discover new forms and traditions consonent with the virgin century. More on that in the next chapter.

Study Questions

1. How did the emergence of an aristocratic court life in the early Renaissance strengthen the development of ballet?
2. Why is the 1581 production of "Ballet Comique de la Royne" recognized as a landmark in the history of dance?
3. The shift from the use of courtiers as performers to that of professional dancers was made during the reign of Louis XIV. What events took place to encourage this important tradition?
4. Name and identify some of the early 18th century stars of the French Ballet.
5. What is *ballet d'action*, and who was responsible for this genre becoming popular?
6. What are the important qualities which denote ballet during the Romantic era?
7. Why is Marie Taglioni one of the singular dancers of the Golden Age? In what ballet did she firmly establish her pre-eminence?
8. What caused the demise of the male dancer during the Romantic period? Name and identify some of the men who managed to achieve success.
9. Why is the name of Marius Petipa synonymous with the emergence of classical ballet in late 19th century Russia?

End Notes

1. Lincoln Kirstein, *Dance: A Short History of Classic Theatrical Dancing,* (New York: Dance Horizons, 1969), pp. 10–11.
2. Ibid., p. 117.
3. Richard Kraus and Sarah Chapman, *History of the Dance in Art and Education,* 2nd ed. (Englewood Cliffs: Prentice-Hall, Inc., 1981), p. 71.
4. Jean George Noverre, *Letters on Dancing and Ballets,* trans. Cyril Beaumont, (New York: Dance Horizons, 1966), p. 104.
5. Ibid., p. 28.
6. Marion Hannah Winter, *The Pre-Romantic Ballet,* (London: Pitman & Sons, 1974), p. 125.
7. Carlo Blasis, *Code of Terpsichore,* trans. R. Barton, (New York: Dance Horizons, n.d.), p. 50.
8. Ibid., p. 52.
9. August Bournonville, *My Theater Life,* trans. Patricia McAndrew, (Middletown, Conn.: Wesleyan University Press, 1979), p. 48.
10. Théophile Gautier, *The Romantic Ballet as Seen through the Eyes of Théophile Gautier,* trans. Cyril Beaumont, (London: C. Beaumont, 1932), p. 9.
11. Alexander Bland, *A History of Ballet and Dance in the Western World,* (London: Barrie & Jenkins Ltd., 1976), p. 64.

Non-classical movements are used in contemporary choreography. Texas Woman's University Dance Repertory Theatre. (Jennifer Collins, photographer)

Ballet in the Twentieth Century · 9

The turn to the 20th century ushered in an era of trauma and excitement. The machine age fostered a sense of personality and independence unheralded in the history of art. Never before had artists felt the need to create unique, individual statements as they have in this century.

Few non-dancers have had so much influence over the course of ballet as Serge Diaghilev (1872–1929). He was, wrote John Percival, "the symbol of what can be achieved by ballet, its power to satisfy the connoisseur and thrill large audiences."[1]

Diaghilev — a Man of Style

Excited by his discovery of the fine arts during his St. Petersburg student years, Diaghilev was seized by a consuming passion for extending his new-found taste upon others. An impressario was born! The man had the requisite skills: part magician, part ego maniac, part diplomat, all textured with a cultured sense of taste, a penchant for novelty, and a spirit of adventure. The year 1897 began with his first exhibition, a modest collection of German and French watercolors. Then he founded Russia's first magazine devoted to art, *The World of Art.*

Always eager to challenge fate, Diaghilev mounted the first exhibition of Russian art to the West in 1906. So successful was it that his plans enlarged to include a group of Russian opera singers on the next tour. In 1909 the entrepreneur substituted the ballet for the fussy singers when they would not come to terms on their contracts.

Called simply the Ballets Russes, these dancers leapt their way into the heart of Parisian cultured society with their miraculous technique and poetry, which to this day still typifies a Russian dancer.

The art of dance had been declining in Paris for some time. Even in Russia, dancers recognized the need to find new ways of expression. Diaghilev said it himself, "What's needed is . . . a movement of liberation in choreography; some fresh form of achievement."[2]

143

A man of great personal drive and immense vision, Diaghilev galvanized a turbulent artistic scene in Paris around a notion of total theater. He did not invent that concept, but he did make it work, popularizing the magnificent theatrical outcomes, making stars, and supporting the new naturalistic choreographic experiments. An arena for the avant garde in art and music as well as the ballet was the exciting result.

Diaghilev's Protegées

Reading like a "Who's Who" list, the recounting of the contributions of Diaghilev's associates emphasizes his ability to single out, nurture, and shape seminal artists.

Michael Fokine (1880–1942)

He graduated from the Imperial Ballet Academy in 1898, already interested in choreographing even while a dancer at the Maryinsky Theater. The idea for his first ballet was rejected in 1904, but later *Daphnis and Chloe* became a success when performed for Diaghilev's troupe in 1912.

Fokine's impressive list of ballets during his nine year tenure with Diaghilev exhibits the full flowering of his creative potential. These ballets represent some of the most remembered treasures from that era of the Ballets Russes.

Chopiana (later renamed "Les Sylphides") in 1909 reflected Fokine's interest in Isadora Duncan's pure dance, inspired by the sensitive soul of Chopin's music. The year 1910 flourished with two other successes, *Le Carnival,* a light ballet d'action with the incomparable Vaslav Nijinsky as Harlequin and Tamara Karsavina as Columbine, then *Scheherazade,* which spawned à la Russe fad fashions. Turbaned ladies slinked from party to party cloaked with visions in their heads of the Golden Slave, danced passionately by Nijinsky.

The Firebird, Fokine's first collaboration with Igor Stravinsky in 1910, captured the essence of Russian folklore in its expressionistic movements. That kind of earthy fantasy succeeded again with *Petrouchka* (1911), relating the pathos of a doll who lives and feels life jolted the dance theater world with its sad ending.

After leaving Ballets Russes, Fokine hopscotched around the world, teaching and restaging his ballets. However, his later works never lived up to his earlier ballets. True to Noverre, Fokine wanted to create new movement for each ballet instead of relying upon stereotyped dance steps found in the studio as had Petipa. He re-examined the use of stylized gesture thereby nourishing the technical foundations of dance.

In every age, there are performers who have charged the theater world with the unique force of their dancing. Technique was not the primary ingredient of their successes; they had a personal style of movement and a charisma that set them apart from their peers. In the 19th century, Marie Taglioni and Auguste Vestris were shining examples. In the early 20th century, the roster included the following Russian dancers.

Even today, over 50 years since he last set foot on a stage, Nijinsky is a legendary standard for excellent male dancing. In 1899, the nine year old Vaslav entered the Imperial Ballet School where he was immediately singled out. He erupted onto the stage like a caged animal, yet an unusual sense of dramatic poetry encompassed his gestures. "As he put on his costume," wrote John Percival, "he seemed to change his placid nature into that of whatever he saw reflected in the mirror."[3]

Diaghilev was to see more than the exceptional dancer in this man. He saw the makings of a choreographer. Stravinsky might complain that Nijinsky knew nothing of meter . . . No matter. *L'apres midi d'un faun* (1912), to a pre-existing Debussey tone poem, created a scandal. Middle class theatergoers' sensibilities were shocked with its suggestiveness and forthright paganism. The following year, *Rite of Spring* was greeted with booing and a full scale riot. Panning the ballet, critics attacked its theme of a primitive sacrificial fertility rite and its emphasis on contracted distortions of the human figure and turned in feet. They called it "anti-ballet" and "satanic."

Unfortunately, the light of sanity was to be snuffed out. After marrying against Diaghilev's wishes, Nijinsky was abruptly dismissed from the company. Reinstated briefly in 1916 for Ballets Russes' American tour, he was

Vaslav Nijinsky (1890–1950)

Fokine's Scheherazade *was a perfect vehicle for Vaslav Nijinsky's cat-like leaps. (Courtesy of the Dance Collection, the New York Public Library at Lincoln Center, Astor, Lenox and Tilden Foundations.)*

committed in 1917, complaining of strange spirits locked inside his head. There, in various European institutions, the great dancer remained until his death in London. Although his candle burned but briefly, few lights were ever so radiant.

Anna Pavlova
(1881–1931)

She re-awakened the Romantic spirit through her highly personalized performing style. The West firsu saw her during her periodic engagements with the Ballets Russes while she was still a member of the Maryinsky Theatre. Diaghilev convinced her to leave Russia, but their association was brief. Her own flamboyancy clashed with the autocraticism of Diaghilev, so she took off on her own in 1911 to form a company to showcase herself.

Thousands flocked to her performances and were inspired by her poetic movements. These extensive tours to the cultural frontiers of the world and her interest in the exotic (she once performed a duet with Indian dancer Udy Shankar) made her a legend. Cyril Beaumont reminisced that Pavlova was "a complete unity in herself, . . . she made her features speak and her body sing."[4]

Russian ballerina, Anna Pavlova, appearing in costume for "The Dying Swan," a solo choreographed by Fokine to Saint Saens music. (Courtesy of the Dance Collection, the New York Public Library at Lincoln Center, Astor, Lenox and Tilden Foundations.)

While Pavlova ignited audiences with her spirit, Karsavina won their admiration with her pure technique and her unparalleled beauty. When she joined Diaghilev's company in 1909, Fokine saw nothing special in her. However, Diaghilev did. So the young ballerina was groomed for stardom.

Much to everyone's surprise, Karsavina possessed a quick mind and acute aesthetic taste. By 1910, she was firmly established as *prima ballerina,* dancing leading roles in *Giselle* and *The Firebird.* "Her own charming personality, fairy-like poetry and ideology never failed to reach across the footlights."[5]

Emigrating to England, a second career awaited the dancer. With her influence, Karsavina was instrumental in establishing an interest in dance in London. Her work as a theoretician and teacher is now better known than her own artistry, and an autobiography, *Theatre Street* (1930), was turned into a successful American film in the late 1970s.

He graduated from the Bolshoi School in Moscow in 1912. Two years later he joined Diaghilev, creating the title role in Michael Fokine's *The Legend of Joseph.* Another creative giant was to be cultivated. Among Massine's most noteworthy works were *Parade* (1917), to a Satie score and Picasso's cubistic costumes, and *The Three Cornered Hat* (1919) to deFalla's music. Both ballets were restaged by Massine in the 1970s for the City Center Robert Joffrey Ballet.

Massine broke away from the Ballets Russes, but in 1932 joined the Ballet Russe de Monte Carlo, a company which attempted to fill the void following Diaghilev's death in 1929.

Massine's most interesting ballets, like *Choreartium* (1934), were experiments in the application of the Delsartian concept of movement flowing directly from the core of the music. In his last years, Massine perfected his theory of composition, wrote, and staged his signature works around the world.

Today, the name Serge Diaghilev has approached deific proportions. As untimely as it was, his death did coincide with a decreased interest in the company and consuming financial, health, and personal problems. It was as if "Fate" had intruded to save the man from tumbling off the pinnacle of success. Loosely based upon his obsessive life was the film, *The Red Shoes,* an inspiration to many young hopefuls. For dancers, the Ballets Russes remains in spirit a symbol of what ballet strives to be in this century: an exciting, entertaining, provoking, total experience absorbing the intellect and emotions.

The London Scene

Two women, both indomitable spirits and forever rivals, were influenced by Diaghilev's willpower and his personal sense of theatrics and taste. They were Ninette de Valois and Marie Rambert, bastions of the English ballet.

Ninette de Valois

An Irish lass born Edris Stannus in 1898, she returned from a trial engagement with the Ballets Russes with a French name to open a ballet school in

Tamara Karsavina (1885–1979)

Leonide Massine (1895–1978)

1926. She joined forces briefly with Marie Rambert and others to found the Camargo Society, an umbrella organization which supported member-produced concerts.

Her strong personality and immense drive made this confederation an impossible situation. Securing Lilian Baylis' support (a director of the Sadler's Wells Theater), de Valois disbanded her academy in 1931 to join forces with Baylis' opera troupe. Performing a repertoire founded upon Russian classical ballets of Petipa, the Vic-Wells Ballet flourished under de Valois' direction.

The ultimate artistic success of the company increased as it began to perform the new ballets created by home-grown choreographers, Frederick Ashton and Kenneth MacMillan. In 1956 Queen Elizabeth retitled the company with an official royal charter: The Royal Ballet. Although retired since 1963, de Valois' pervasive spirit floats over the company.

Ashton's most notable works for The Royal Ballet include *Ondine* (1958) with the incomparable Margot Fonteyn (his muse) in her prime; a spritely reconstruction of Jean Dauberval's *La Fille mal Gardée* (1960); *The Dream* (1964) based upon Skakespeare's play; a starkly modernistic *Monotones* (1965); and a reflective *A Month in the Country* (1976). A craftsman, Ashton submerges himself and the dancers fully into his ballets. "Few choreographers have surrendered themselves to dance with such total abandon," wrote Margot Fonteyn.[6]

Marie Rambert
(1880–1982)

She changed her name also, from the Polish Cyvia Rambom. Trained in Warsaw, she was enflamed by Jacques Dalcroze's theories in 1910, soon becoming his assistant. Her encounter with Diaghilev occurred when she was engaged to assist Nijinsky's creating of *Rite of Spring,* also to dance in the corps. Back in London where she, like de Valois, opened a school in 1920, Ballet Rambert was organized in 1935. As a pioneer of the dance, Rambert is still known for her readiness to take chances.

Ballet Rambert, with its contemporary barefoot repertoire and ensemble unity, functions today as a sharp contrast to the traditional Royal Ballet. "In the beginning it showed the way," wrote Mary Clarke, "now it shows the other point of view."[7] She was a nurturer of many of the most noteworthy 20th century choreographers, like Ashton, Antony Tudor, Agnes de Mille, and John Cranko. While Tudor (born in 1908) made a name for himself in America with his psychologically tense dances, Cranko excelled in narrative composition, such as *Eugene Onegin* (1965) and *The Taming of the Shrew* (1969). His ballets sky-rocketed the German Stuttgart Ballet onto the international scene until he was struck down by a heart attack in 1973.

Back to Russia

The Revolution of 1917 scattered dancers in fear of political reprisals to the West seeking a new life. Filling this artistic void required organized, systematic leadership. Thus the way was paved for the single greatest Russian contribution to the art of ballet since the neo-classic revival led by Marius Petipa

40 years earlier. Agrippina Vaganova (1879–1951), one of the greatest pedagogues of all time, emerged. Her gifts were not so much as a dancer, although ballerina status was achieved in 1915. Instead, Vaganova excelled as an analyzer of balletic movement. She picked apart other teaching styles, like that of Enrico Cecchetti, to discover the pure central core of classical alignment, line, balance, and energy.

Vaganova's discoveries led to the total reorganization of the teaching process in Russia and, through emigrés to the West, her principles have influenced teaching methods throughout the world. Post-Revolutionary Soviet dancers quickly attained extraordinary virtuosity without losing an inherent poetic Russian spirit.

Another major influence on ballet training in America has been the artist-teacher, Enrico Cecchetti (1850–1928), a spritely Italian virtuoso who created both the technically demanding Bluebird and the forbidding mime role Carabosse for Petipa's masterpiece, *Sleeping Beauty* (1890).

Until 1910, when he too was engaged by Diaghilev, the Maestro contributed greatly to the technical improvement of the Maryinsky Theatre dancers with his training concepts. He analyzed the technical qualities which dancers must attain and then presented the techniques in a graduated manner. He felt that three natural gifts were imperative in the making of a ballerina: strength, elevation, and turning ability.

Most teachers of dance in the United States were touched by the descendants of both Vaganova and Cecchetti. It is upon their contributions to the teaching of ballet that all contemporary training methods are based.

Two major Russian companies are known best to American audiences because they have toured the West in recent years. The Kirov Ballet in Leningrad, renown for its Maryinsky heritage of purity in line, form, and musicality, is situated in the cultural center of Russia. The Bolshoi, literally meaning *big,* in Moscow reflects the more political, industrial center of the Soviet Union in its bold, physical style.

Since the ballet in Russia (along with other arts) was put to work publicizing the new regime, educating the masses, and establishing a new moral ethic called social realism, development of a solid choreographic base has advanced slowly. In such ballets as the nationalistic *The Red Poppy* (1927), creativity and craftsmanship have taken second place to pyrotechnics and moralistic messages.

Dancers defecting from such narrow artistic guidelines have influenced the development of dance in the West, particularly in the United States. For one thing, the publicity alone has made ballet almost a household word. And for another, dancers like Rudolf Nureyev, Natalia Makarova, Mikhail Baryshnikov, and Alexander Godounov have injected Western ballet with higher performance standards and a certain emotional quality not seen previously. Russian companies have changed, too. For one thing, the dancers are thinner and more lithe. And for another, choreographic experimentation has begun to occur such as at the Maly Theater in Moscow.

And Back
to Copenhagen

As mentioned in the previous chapter, The Royal Danish Ballet flourished throughout the life of August Bournonville, continuing in an unbroken line to this day, making it one of the oldest ballet companies in the world. Following Bournonville's death in 1879, his successors have attempted to retain Bournonville's French Romantic legacy and rich choreography. One of the most successful was Hans Beck (1861–1952) who edited and re-arranged whole sections of Bournonville's ballets to make the works more palatable to Danish working class audiences.

Codified were what could be remembered of Bournonville's classes, including snippets of the choreography. What resulted is known today as the Bournonville Schools, lessons for six days of the week.

Harald Lander (1905–1971) introduced the Danes to Russian technique in the 1930s. Best remembered for his academically classical blockbuster *Étude* (1948), Lander later went on to assume the artistic directorship of first the Paris Opera and then American Ballet Theatre before retiring in Paris.

In later years, Fleming Flindt (1936) and Henning Kronstam (1934) have served as artistic directors. While the former, now artistic director of the Dallas Ballet, was known for his own flamboyantly dramatic works and his dabbling into the modern barefoot idiom, the latter was a leading *premier danseur noble* of his generation, not a choreographer at all. Returning newly re-staged productions of Bournonville's ballets to the repertoire has been Kronstam's special mission.

The Royal Danish Ballet is probably best known for its male dancers, some who have "defected" to American companies. Foremost was Erik Bruhn, in whose biography John Gruen has called "one of the twentieth century's

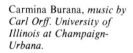

Carmina Burana, music by Carl Orff. University of Illinois at Champaign-Urbana.

greatest classical male dancers." In 1964, seeing the need to develop depth in his male dancers, George Balanchine hired Stanley Williams to head the training for the New York City Ballet. Since then, a steady trickle of Scandinavians have made their way across the Atlantic to find fame in America: Helgi Tomasson, Peter Martins, Adam Lüders, and Ib Andersen, among them.

One of the last ballet masters to work for Diaghilev was a brash, 20 year old dancer-choreographer. News had spread about his underground experimental ballets in Leningrad. Diaghilev was intrigued. Sidelined in 1927 by an injury, the young man nevertheless developed choreographically during his almost five years with Ballets Russes.

Ballet in America
New York City
Ballet

In 1933 Lincoln Kirstein, a young American balletomane, attached himself to this young man. He wanted to start a company, one with a particularly American brand of choreography, much as Petipa's ballets had reflected Russian taste and spirit. It was time to have ballet take root in the United States, not as a transplant, but as a vital, indigenous art form.

That young man was George Balanchine! The rest is history, although certainly not the fairy tale kind. The company struggled first to gain an audience, then a permanent home, and always to achieve a firm financial footing. Of singular note is the fact that the New York City Ballet was the first company since Petipa's tenure with the Imperial Ballet in Russia in which one individual alone was responsible for the entire repertoire. "Balanchine's ambition has ever been to make audiences see sound and hear dancing."[8]

Balanchine's neo-classical style was first seen in Stravinsky's *Apollon Musagete* (1928), since restaged under the name *Apollo*. It was a work tightly bound to the rhythmic and phrasing concepts set out in the score. Besides his dedication to a strong musical foundation, Balanchine's choreography has been known for its dedication to ensemble dancing and its consuming interest in the femaleness (as opposed to femininity) of the dance. Notable ballets representing a variety of things include: *Serenade* (1934), *Mozartiana* (revised in 1981), *Symphony in C* (1947), *Concerto Barocco* (1941), *Jewels* (1967), and the perennial Christmas favorite *The Nutcracker* (1954).

Balanchine exerted an exacting influence over the growth and development of ballet in America. His choreography is performed throughout the United States by small and large companies alike. And his unique style has had considerable influence over both training methods and choreographic style to such an extent that Europeans call it "American."

Jerome Robbins (1918). The associate director of the New York City Ballet is just about everyone's favorite choreographer. Whether it be in his successful excursions into the jazz or musical comedy genres, such as his *West Side Story* and *Fiddler on the Roof*, or his innovative free-style choreographic approach like *Interplay* (1945) and *Dances at a Gathering* (1969), Robbins caught the aesthetics of his age at its apex. His one act ballets have been fresh in their challenge to one's taste and spiritual sensitivity. *Afternoon of a Faun* (1953), for instance, was indelibly associated with the Nijinsky ballet. But, Robbins stepped in and rediscovered in the music a tense study of the uncanny ability dancers have in masking their innermost personal selves behind the wall of the studio and in blocking out reality with the inherent narcissism of the mirror.

Balanchine's death in 1983 ended a fertile era in American ballet. Longtime danseur noble, Peter Martins, known for his impeccable classical line and Nordic coolness of manner, emerged in recent years as a choreographer. He acknowledged unashamedly Balanchine's guiding hand for his early works like *Calcium Night Light* (1979) and *Symphony #1* (1981). Martins has retired as a dancer to direct the New York City Ballet, a company he adopted when the Danish dancer joined it in 1969 then only 23 years old.

American Ballet Theatre

Entirely different has been the development of American Ballet Theatre. Founded in 1939, it metamorphosed into its present structure and name in 1945 under the co-directorship of wealthy dancer, Lucia Chase, and reputed scenic designer, Oliver Smith. Over the years, the company's artistic policies have been energetic and persistently eclectic. Often accused of sacrificing neatness in performance for dramatic elaboration, ABT has been committed to a diverse repertoire created by its own choreographers. The company relished being a forum for different creative philosophies. Works depicting contemporary psychological thoughts and those addressing American themes were once encouraged.

Eugene Loring (1914–1982). In his *Billy the Kid* (1939) with its Aaron Copland score, Loring strove to incorporate modern and natural movement into a classical model. Other choreographers were also experimenting with themes involving interpersonal relationships.

Antony Tudor (1908). *Pillar of Fire* (1942) is a work best exemplifying Tudor's taut psychological portraiture, while *Jardin aux Lilas* (1936) is a comment on polite social mores. As a choreographer of human sorrow, his later works, such as *The Leaves are Fading* (1975), brush man against fate and force a deeper psychological insight into the darker parts of his soul.

Agnes deMille (1909). One of the few noteworthy female choreographers to emerge in the history of ballet so far, deMille developed her creative temperament with ABT. Selma Jeanne Cohen has called her primary works, *Rodeo* (1942) and *Fall River Legend* (1948), harshly realistic yet not without humor and poetry. "She is the master of expressionistic Americana."[9] Besides choreographing for both the concert stage and Broadway, Miss deMille is a vocal, articulate lobbyist for the arts and a respected popular author on dance: *Dance to the Piper* (1952), *Book of the Dance* (1963), and *America Dancing* (1980).

Formerly a hot bed for creative experimentation, ABT has more recently become a mecca for world famous defectors. All the major Russians previ-

Dancers in performance. Brigham Young University Theatre Ballet.

ously mentioned have found a ready home with the company; Mikhail Barishnikov, still a vital performer, even moved into the retired Lucia Chase's office as artistic director, thereby reforming the corps and the repertoire on more traditional classical models.

The Chamber-Sized Company

City Center Joffrey Ballet

In 1956, Robert Joffrey piled into a station wagon with six dancers and a neat package of contemporary-oriented ballets. Now the City Center Joffrey Ballet has celebrated its 25th anniversary as America's oldest medium-sized company. Owing its longevity to its bright, exciting repertoire choreographed primarily by Gerald Arpino, the Joffrey Ballet has endured through numerous financial crises by keeping a keen eye glued to the hip trends of its modish audiences.

A carefully planned repertoire of contemporary ballets has been developed and includes Arpino's *Trinity* (1971), Twyla Tharp's *Deuce Coupe* (1973), and William Forsythe's *Love Songs* (1983). Balancing this diet has been a healthy serving of nearly forgotten masterpieces, like August Bournonville's *Konservatoriet* (1849), Leonide Massine's *Parade* (1917), and Kurt Jooss' *The Green Table* (1932).

Dance Theatre of Harlem

The Dance Theatre of Harlem represents another grand experiment in contemporary ballet history: an all-black company born in a Harlem church basement, which debuted in 1971. Germinated from the seeds of Arthur Mitchell's personal commitment following the assassination of Martin Luther King, this company has matured into one of America's most exciting troupes. Fertilized with the unquestioned instincts, vision, and the diligence of its director (the first black American danseur noble) as well as the artistic generosity of the dance community, a Balanchine neo-classical influence is undeniable. Yet there is an ethnicity also, owing to its popular, jazz-oriented repertoire.

Eliot Feld Ballet

A third kind of company to emerge is best exemplified in the evolution of the Eliot Feld Ballet. Founded originally as the American Ballet Company in 1969 by the acknowledged protegée of Jerome Robbins, it disbanded plagued by financial crises. Reawakened in 1974, the Feld Ballet is the performing show-case of one of the few young choreographers to achieve major stature since the 1950s.

While still in the corps de ballet of American Ballet Theatre, Feld burst onto the scene with his tight, carefully modeled *Harbinger* (1967) to Prokofiev music. "Feld's musicality is without blemish," wrote Agnes deMille. "His style is ravishing and quite unmatched for one so young."[10] His ballets often deal with lonely individuals set against masses of busyness and repetition of move-ment phrases.

A Last Word

In the last 20 years, America has experienced an explosion in the number of dance companies and dance performances being presented. Americans have discovered expression through motion, eager to experience visual stimulation and to develop sensory appreciation. The mysticism of seeing a dancer chal-lenge space as he attempts to reject the laws of gravity in a grand jeté of magic-like effortlessness has become totally irresistible. According to a recent Harris poll, more Americans attend theater and other culturally related events each year than attend all sporting events put together.

There is now understood to be an artist in each of us, with a unique mode of expression vested in our ability to perceive kinetically and respond to our environment without the necessity for verbal information or interaction: our own humanity. There is an exhilaration from the very act of moving which creates a powerful sense of presence in which one's mind, body, and spirit are freed to interrelate harmoniously.

Your own study of ballet will unlock secret energies and potentialities for self analysis and discovery. You will learn through your own personal inves-tigations to appreciate the historical pathway you have just completed in these last two chapters. The very technical precepts which you will examine and practice along with the artistic nuances of gesture have all evolved from the various inputs people have made through the years.

Beyond merely learning new posture habits, step patterns, and acquiring a movement vocabulary, dance really is a magical phenomenon. It calls you like the mysterious "black hole" in space, and the results will forever change your perception of yourself. As a constant challenge, your dance experiences will lead you to new levels of personal enrichment and growth.

Study Questions

1. Serge Diaghilev was a man with a special mission. Why do we mark his accomplishments as a turning point in the history of dance?
2. Name and identify three choreographers encouraged by Diaghilev for his company, the Ballets Russes.
3. What contributions did the following early 20th century dancers make to ballet: Anna Pavlova and Vaslav Nijinsky?
4. Who were the two women responsible for creating the first permanent ballet companies in England? Name their companies.
5. Name the two most notable choreographers to emerge in England. Name and describe two of their works.
6. How has Agnes deMille contributed to the enrichment of dance?
7. We remember a Russian woman and an Italian man for the teaching of classical ballet in this century. Name them and describe their work.
8. Identify the two primary Russian companies.
9. With which American company was George Balanchine associated?
10. How does American Ballet Theatre differ from the New York City Ballet?
11. Of the other companies described, name one of them and describe its work.

End Notes

1. John Percival, *The World of Diaghilev,* (New York: E. P. Dutton & Co., 1971), p. 149.
2. Ibid., p. 89.
3. Ibid., p. 24.
4. Parmenia Migel, *The Ballerinas,* (New York: MacMillan, 1972), p. 271.
5. Peter Lieven, *The Birth of the Ballets-Russes,* (New York: Dover Publications, Inc., 1973), p. 329.
6. Margot Fonteyn, *Margot Fonteyn,* (New York: Alfred A. Knopf, 1976).
7. Mary Clarke, *Dancers of Mercury,* (London: Adam and Chas. Black, Ltd., 1962), p. 272.
8. Bernard Taper, *Balanchine,* (New York: Harper & Row, 1963), p. 161.
9. Selma Jeanne Cohen, ed., *Dictionary of Modern Ballet,* (New York: Tudor Publishing Co., 1959), p. 115.
10. Agnes deMille, *America Dancing,* (New York: MacMillan Publishing Co., 1980), p. 180.

Appendix

List of Standard Body Facings and Movement Directions

Croisé derrière—crossed to a back diagonal.

Croisé devant—crossed to a front diagonal.

Derrière, à la quatrième—straight behind.

Devant, à la quatrième—straight in front.

Écarté—standing on an oblique line to the audience; meaning—spread, separated, or open.

Éffacé derrière—open on a back diagonal.

Éffacé devant—open on a front diagonal.

Seconde, à la—to the side.

Arrière, en—traveling backwards (can be combined with éffacé and croisé).

Avant, en—traveling forward (can be combined with éffacé and croisé).

Dedans, en—circling or turning inward toward the center line of gravity.

Dehors, en—circling or turning outward away from the center line of gravity.

De côté—traveling sideward.

Dessous—transferring weight under the supporting foot.

Dessus—transferring weight over the supporting foot.

En croix—exercises performed to the front—side—back—side.

En l'air—in the air.

En menage—traveling around the room in a circle.

Glossary

Abaisé lowering from demi pointe without going into demi plié.

Adagio slow, lyrical movements performed to develop strength, line, and control.

Alignment body posture in which the various segments are placed or held efficiently close to the center line of gravity.

Allegro brisk, bright tempo; a category for combinations of movements usually involving turns, small jumps, and beats.

Allegro, grand a category for large leaps and jumps which emphasizes strength, coordination, and a controlled use of demi plié.

Arabesque a primary pose in ballet in which the dancer stands on one leg with the other fully extended behind.

Assemblé a jump or relevé preceded by a dégagé in which the working leg closes or assembles to a tight 5th position.

Assemblé soutenu see soutenu en dedans en tournant.

Attitude a pose in which the dancer balances on one leg while bending the other from 45°–90°. Can be done with leg held behind or in front of the body.

Au milieu center practice.

Balancé, pas step pattern related to the waltz; perform three steps (down-up-down); may be used as a preparation.

Ballerina literally a female dancer, but generally used to refer to a dancer of the soloist rank.

Ballet a dance choreographed for the theater blending balletic movement, accompaniment, and decor—costumes, scenery, and lighting.

Ballon a light, springy quality in jumping.

Ballonné a bouncy-like hop in which the working leg does a dégagé in a given direction and closes to sur le cou de pied on the fondu landing.

Barre the hand railing about 40″ from the floor which is used for support during the first part of the lesson.

Battement fondu to melt; a controlled plié usually on one leg.

Battement frappé a sharply brushed battement performed from sur le cou de pied position to the front, side, and back directions.

Battement glissé a battement tendu performed in a gliding quality usually including a demi plié.

Battement relevé beating raised.

Battement tendu a primary action of barre work in which the foot stretches from a closed position outward, keeping the knee straight, until the foot is fully pointed with only the tips of the toes contacting the floor.

Cambré bending the torso in any direction from the waist.

Chaîné literally a chain; successive turns in which the dancer remains in 1st position on demi pointe throughout.

Changement des pieds a jump which changes the feet.

Chassé literally to chase; a sliding action performed in any direction.

Choreographer the inventor or creator of dances.

Ciseaux a changement in which the feet open to 2nd position, a scissors action.

Contretemps, demi a step combining a hop (temps levé) and a slide (chassé) to any direction.

Cou de pied, sur le literally on the neck of the foot; a position on one leg in which the working foot is held extended at the ankle of the supporting leg.

Coupé a slicing or cutting action in which the weight transfers abruptly from one foot to the other.

Croisé crossed; a direction or pose in which the legs appear to cross each other; the opposite of éffacé. One of the 8 traditional body facing directions.

De côté traveling in a sideward direction.

Dégagé to disengage the working foot by extending it to about 45°.

Demi pointe standing on the balls of the feet with heels lifted as high as possible.

Derrière, à la quatrième to the 4th position in back; one of the 8 traditional body facing directions.

Dessous transferring weight or closing the foot in back or under.

Dessus transferring weight or closing the foot in front or over.

Devant, à la quatrième to the 4th position in front; one of the 8 traditional body facing directions.

Développé an unfolding action of the leg from 5th position to the desired extended height.

Écarté spread; one of the 8 traditional body facing directions in which the foot points to 2nd position, but the body is facing at an angle to the audience.

Échappé literally to escape; a jump beginning in 5th position and springing up so that the feet open to 2nd or 4th position. On the next jump, the feet return to 5th position. Can also be performed on a relevé.

Éffacé shaded; the direction of movement or pose in which the legs appear open and the body is at an angle to the audience. The opposite of croisé. One of the 8 traditional body facing directions.

Elevé a controlled rising to demi pointe.

En arrière traveling backward.

En avant traveling forward.

En bas low, the lowest position of the arms.

En croix in the shape of a cross; an exercise performed forward, sideward, backward, and sideward in sequence.

En dedans turning or circling toward the center line of gravity; the opposite of en dehors.

En dehors turning or circling away from the center line of gravity; the opposite of en dedans.

En haut overhead pose in which the arms are in 5th position.

Épaulement literally shouldering; the subtle movements of the upper torso, shoulders, including changes in focus which enhance shapes, lines, and designs in movement.

Facing Directions of the Body traditionally, the dancer faces and moves in 8 directions established to create attractive body lines within the context of a proscenium style stage space. See Appendix.

Failli To give way; similar to a demi contretemps except that the back leg releases to a demi arabesque on the hop followed by that leg sliding through 1st position to croisé devant.

Fondu see battement fondu.

Frappé see battement frappé.

Glissade to glide; a primary action in dance. Can be performed in any direction.

Glissé see battement glissé.

Grand battement a high, straight leg beat, a lifting action, performed to any of the body directional facings: devant, écarté, seconde, derrière.

Grand battement en clôche a series of large beats progressing front and back with the foot brushing carefully through 1st position; a pendulum action. Torso remains vertical.

Grand battement lent a slow extension of the leg from 5th position to the desired height.

Jeté a leap, beginning either from one or two feet and landing on one foot. May be preceded by a brushing action. Can be performed in any direction.

Jeté, grand a large leap in which the leading leg does a grand battement propelling the dancer into the air.

Jeté simple a jeté in which the dancer springs vertically and changes feet without the usual brushing action.

Marché, pas walking forward or backward by leading with a fully extended foot in an elegant, courtly manner.

Pas de basque a folk step in 3 beats in which the dancer executes a demi rond de jambe and steps to the side (ct. 1), slides the next foot through 1st position (ct. 2), and steps forward (ct. 3), ending in pointe tendue derrière; can also be performed backward.

Pas de bourré a traditional movement pattern from court dancing involving 3 steps (up-up-down). Can be performed in many directions either by itself or as a preparation.

Pas de bourré en tournant a pas de bourré which either turns en dehors (outward, away from the supporting leg) or en dedans (inward, toward the supporting leg). Do ½ or a whole turn during the 3 steps of each pas de bourré.

Pas de chat step of the cat; a leap in which successive passé are performed, first lifting the leg leading into the direction of the step.

Passé a retiré which lifts higher to allow toe tips to touch the side of the knee before closing with the other foot in 5th front position.

Petit battement small beats performed sur le cou de pied.

Piqué to prick; a quick step onto a straight supporting leg in which the working leg is held in a specific position. Can be performed as a turn either towards the direction of the supporting leg or away from it.

Pirouette a relevé spin on one leg. The turn may be done either en dehors or en dedans.

Plié, demi bending the knees slightly, used as a preparation for almost every step.

Plié, grand a deep knee bend in which (except for 2nd position) the heels release from the floor.

Pointe dancing performed by women on the tips of their toes with the aid of specially made satin shoes in which the toes are supported by blocking, a stiffening of the ends of the shoes.

Pointe tendue a pose holding battement tendue position.

Port de bras carriage of the arms usually combined with épaulement and cambré.

Port de corps carriage of the body; exercises to relax and increase the flexibility of the spine.

Porté to carry, a jump which travels horizontally in space.

Posé see piqué.

Premier danseur literally first male dancer; used today to label the leading male soloist.

Retiré withdrawing the foot abruptly from the floor up the calf to a position under the knee.

Révérence a courtly bow usually performed at the end of a lesson.

Rond de jambe à terre a straight legged circling action of the leg in which the foot remains in contact with the floor.

Rond de jambe en l'air beginning with the leg extended to 2nd position, an elliptical circling action of the toe inward to touch the knee of the supporting leg which is complete when the leg re-extends to 2nd position.

Rond de jambe, grand a straight legged circling action of the leg off the floor.

Sauté a jump, taking off from either one or two feet and landing on both feet.

Seconde, à la sideward extension of the arms and legs; one of the 8 traditional body facing directions.

Sissonne fermé while springing from 2 feet perform a strong battement with the leg opposite to the direction in which the dancer is traveling, then quickly close the extended foot upon landing. Can be performed forward, backward, and sideward.

Sissonne ouverte spring from 2 feet with the leg opposite to that direction performing a strong battement. Land in fondu, holding the extension momentarily before closing to 5th position. Can be performed forward, sideward, and backward.

Sissonne simple spring from two feet and land on one with the working foot held in sur le cou de pied.

Soubresaut a jump into the air holding the legs in a tight 5th position (sous-sus). The jump moves slightly forward, sideward, or backward.

Sous-sus a pose in which the dancer does a posé or a piqué forward immediately closing the other foot to a tight 5th position on pointe. Also done with a relevé from a demi plié; can be performed in directions other than the one described.

Soutenu en dedans en tournant commonly called soutenu tour; a fundamental cross-over pivot turn. Also known as assemblé soutenu.

Spotting a trick of snapping the focus and head during a turn to help diminish dizziness and clarify the turn.

Studio the room equipped with mirrors and barres in which dance classes and rehearsals for ballets are held.

Temps levé to hop on one foot.

Temps lié a smooth connecting step pattern in which weight is transferred through an undercurve demi plié action.

Tombé, pas a falling action onto a controlled demi plié.

Bibliography

Ballet News, Metropolitan Opera Guild, 1865 Broadway, New York, N.Y. 10023. **Periodicals**
Dancemagazine, 33 W. 60th St., New York, N.Y. 10023.
Dance News, 1965 Broadway, New York, N.Y. 10023.

Beaumont, Cyril and Stanislas Idzikowski. *A Manual of the Theory and Practice of* **Technical Manuals**
    Classical Theatrical Dancing (rev. ed.). London: C. W. Beaumont, 1971.
Blasis, Carlo. *An Elementary Treatise upon the Theory and Practice of the Art of*
    Dancing, trans. Mary Stewart Evans (orig. 1820). New York: Dover
    Publications, Inc., 1968.
Bruhn, Erik. *Bournonville and Ballet Technique.* New York: The MacMillan Co.,
    1961.
Hammond, Sandra. *Ballet Basics,* 2nd ed. Palo Alto, California: Mayfield Press,
    1984.
Hammond, Sandra. *Beyond Ballet Basics.* Palo Alto, California: Mayfield Press,
    1981.
Karasavina, Tamara. *Ballet Technique.* New York: Theatre Arts Books, 1956.
Karasavina, Tamara. *Classical Ballet: The Flow of Movement.* New York: The
    MacMillan Co., 1962.
Lawson, Joan. *The Teaching of Classical Ballet.* 2nd ed. New York: Theatre Arts
    Books, 1984.
Prudhomme, Germaine. *The Book of Ballet,* trans. Katherine Corsan. Englewood
    Cliffs, N.J.: Prentice-Hall, 1976.
Vaganova, Agrippina. *Basic Principles of Classical Ballet,* trans. Anatole Chujoy.
    New York: Dover Publications, Inc., 1969.

Alter, Judy. *Surviving Exercise: Judy Alter's Safe and Sane Exercise Program.* **Care of the Body**
    Boston; Houghton Mifflin Co., 1983.
Dunn, Beryl. *Dance! Therapy for Dancers.* London: Heineman Health Books, 1974.
Gelabert, Raoul. *Anatomy for the Dancer, vol. I.* New York: Dancemagazine, 1964.
Gelabert, Raoul. *Anatomy for the Dancer, vol. II.* New York: Dancemagazine,
    1966.

Paskevska, Anna. *Both Sides of the Mirror: The Science and Art of Ballet.* New York: Dance Horizons, 1981.

Sparger, Celia. *Anatomy and Ballet.* London: A. & C. Black, Ltd., 1965.

Sweigard, Lulu. *Human Movement Potential, Its Ideokinetic Facilitation.* New York: Dodd, Mead & Co., 1974.

Vincent, L. M. *The Dancer's Book of Health.* Kansas City: Sheed Andrews & McMeel, Inc., 1979.

Dictionaries and References

Beaumont, Cyril. *Complete Book of Ballet.* Garden City, N.J.: Garden City Publishing Co., 1941.

Clarke, Mary and David Vaughan. *The Encyclopedia of Dance and Ballet.* New York: Putnam, 1977.

Grant, Gail. *Technical Manual and Dictionary of Classical Ballet,* (rev. ed.). New York: Dover Publications, Inc., 1983.

Keogler, Horst. *The Concise Oxford Dictionary of Ballet,* 2nd ed. London: Oxford University Press, 1982.

Reynolds, Nancy. *The Dance Catalog.* New York: Harmony Books, 1979.

The Simon and Schuster Book of Ballet. New York: Simon and Schuster, 1979.

History

Anderson, Jack. *Dance.* New York: Newsweek Books, 1974.

Anderson, Jack. *The One and Only: The Ballet Russe de Monte Carlo.* New York: Dance Horizons, 1981.

Aschengreen, Erik. "The Beautiful Danger: Facets of the Romantic Ballet," *Dance Perspectives,* 1974.

Beaumont, Cyril. *Serge Diaghilev.* London: C. W. Beaumont, 1933.

Beaumont, Cyril. *Ballet Design: Past and Present.* New York: Studio Publications, 1946.

Beaumont, Cyril. *The Ballet Called "Giselle."* New York: Dance Horizons, 1969.

Bland, Alexander. *The History of Ballet in the Western World.* New York: Praeger, 1976.

Bland, Alexander. *The Royal Ballet: The First Fifty Years.* Garden City, N.J.: Doubleday & Co., 1981.

Bournonville, August. *My Theater Life,* trans. Patricia McAndrew (orig. 1848). Middletown, PA: Wesleyan University Press, 1979.

Brinson, Peter. *Ballet and Dance: A Guide to the Repertory.* North Pomet, VT: David & Charles, 1980.

Clarke, Mary. *Ballet Art: from Renaissance to the Present.* New York: Clarkson & Potter, Inc., 1978.

Clare, Mary. *The History of Dance.* New York: Crown Publishers, 1981.

Cohen, Selma Jeanne, ed. *Dance as a Theatre Art.* New York: Dodd, Mead & Co., 1974.

Crisp, Clement and Edward Thorpe. *The Colorful World of Ballet.* London: Octopus Books, 1977.

Doeser, Linda. *Ballet and Dance: The World's Major Companies.* New York: St. Martin's Press, 1977.

Gautier, Théophile. *The Romantic Ballet as Seen by Théophile Gautier,* trans. Cyril Beaumont (orig. 1943). London: C. W. Beaumont, 1973.

Guest, Ivor. *Victorian Ballet Girl*. London: A. & C. Black, 1957.

Hilton, Wendy. *Dance of Court and Theater: The French Nobel Style, 1690–1725*. Princeton, N.J.: Princton Book Co., 1981.

Kirstein, Lincoln. *The New York City Ballet*. New York: Alfred Knopf, 1973.

Kraus, Richard and Sarah Chapman. *History of the Dance in Art and Education*, 2nd ed. Englewood Cliffs, N.J.: Prentice-Hall, Inc., 1981.

Lawson, Joan. *The Story of Ballet*. New York: Pitman Publishing Co., 1976.

Moore, Lillian. *Echoes of American Ballet*. Brooklyn: Dance Horizons, 1976.

Noverre, Jean Georges, trans. C. W. Beaumont. *Letters on Dancing and the Ballet* (orig. Engl. 1951). New York: Dance Horizons Reprint, 1968.

Palmer, Winthrop. *Theatrical Dancing in America: The Development of the Ballet from 1900*. New York: B. Ackerman, 1945.

Percival, John. *Modern Ballet*. London: Studio Vista, 1970.

Slonimsky, Juri, et. al. *The Soviet Ballet* (orig. 1947). New York: DeCapo Press, 1970.

Sorrell, Walter. *Dance in Its Time*. Garden City, N.J.: Anchor Press, 1981.

Stevens, Franklin. *Dance as Life: A Season with ABT*. New York: Harper & Row, 1976.

Swift, Mary Grace. *The Art of Dance in the U.S.S.R.* Notre Dame: University of Notre Dame, 1968.

Terry, Walter. *Dance in America*. New York: Harper & Row, 1956.

Winter, Marion Hannah. *The Pre-Romantic Ballet*. New York: Pitman Publishing Corp., 1974.

Biographies

Baryshnikov, Mikhail. *Baryshnikov at Work*. New York: Alfred Knopf, 1976.

Beaumont, Cyril. *Three French Dancers of the Eighteenth Century: Camargo, Salle, Guimard*. London: C. W. Beaumont, 1934.

Beaumont, Cyril. *Michel Fokine and His Ballets* (orig. 1945). New York: Dance Horizons, 1981.

Bland, Alexander. *Fonteyn & Nureyev*. New York: Times Books, 1979.

DeMille, Agnes. *Dance to the Piper*. Boston: Little, Brown & Co., 1952.

Fokine, Michel. *Fokine: Memoirs of a Ballet Master*. Boston: Little, Brown & Co., 1961.

Guest, Ivor. *Fanny Cerrito: The Life of a Romantic Ballerina*, 2nd ed. London: Dance Books, Ltd., 1974.

Hayden, Melissa. *Melissa Hayden, Off Stage and On*. New York: Doubleday & Co., 1963.

Kahn, Albert E. *Days with Ulanova*. New York: Simon & Schuster, 1962.

Karasavina, Tamara. *Theatre Street*, (rev. ed.), (orig. 1930). London: W. Heinemann, Ltd., 1950.

Kirstein, Lincoln. *Nijinsky Dancing*. New York: Alfred Knopf, 1975.

Lazzarini, John. *Pavlova: A Repertoire of a Legend*. New York: Schirmer Books, 1980.

Lifar, Serge. *Serge Diaghilev: His Life, His Work, His Legend* (orig. 1940). New York: DaCapo Press, 1976.

Makarova, Dina. *Natalia Makarova*. Brooklyn: Dance Horizons, 1975.

Massine, Leonide. Ed. Phyllis Hartnoll & Robert Rubens. *My Life in Ballet*. New York: St. Martin's Press, 1969.

Migel, Parmenia. *The Ballerinas: From the Court of Louis XIV to Pavlova*. New York: The MacMillan Co., 1972.

Percival, John. *Nureyev: Aspects of the Dancer*. New York: Putnam, 1975.

Taper, Bernard. *Balanchine* (rev. ed.). New York: MacMillan Publishing Co., 1974.

Appreciation and Aesthetics

Ambrose, Kay. *The Ballet-lover's Companion* (orig. 1943). New York: A. A. Knopf, 1973.

Austin, Richard. *Images of the Dance*. London: Vison, 1975.

Balanchine, George. Ed. Franics Mason. *Balanchine's Complete Stories of the Great Ballets*. Garden City: Doubleday & Co., 1977.

Brinson, Peter. *Ballet for All*. London: Pan Books, 1970.

Buckle, Richard, *Buckle at the Ballet: Selected Criticism*. New York: Atheneum, 1980.

Cartwright, Hilary. *Dancing for a Living: Ballet and Contemporary Dance*. Reading, PA: Educational Explorers, 1974.

Clarke, Mary and Clement Crisp. *Making a Ballet*. New York: The MacMillan Co., 1974.

Clarke, Mary and Clement Crisp. *Understanding Ballet*. New York: Harmony Books, 1976.

Croce, Arlene. *Afterimages*. New York: Alfred Knopf, 1977.

Denby, Edwin. *Looking at the Dance*. New York: Horizon Press, 1968.

Gruen, John. *The Private World of Ballet*. New York: Viking Press, 1975.

Haskell, Arnold. *Balletomania Then and Now*. New York: A. A. Knopf, 1977.

Mazo, Joseph. *Dance Is a Contact Sport*. New York: Saturday Review Press, 1974.

Monahan, James. *The Nature of Ballet: A Critic's Reflections*. London: Pitman Publishing Corp., 1976.

Moore, Lillian. *Echoes of American Ballet: A Collection of Seventeen Articles*. Brooklyn: Dance Horizons, 1976.

Newman, Barbara. *Striking a Balance: Dancers Talk about Dancing*. Boston; Houghton Mifflin, 1982.

Philp, Richard and Mary Whitney. *Danseur: The Male in Ballet*. New York: McGraw Hill, 1977.

Siegel, Marcia. *At the Vanishing Point. A Critic Looks at Dance*. New York: Saturday Review Press, 1972.

Stevens, Franklin. *Dance as Life: A Season with the American Ballet Theatre*. New York: Harper & Row, 1976.

Terry, Walter. *How to Look at Dance*. New York: Morrow, 1982.

Index